The All-Rounder

Also in the Sporting Skills Series

PACE BOWLING   Bob Willis
WICKETKEEPING   Bob Taylor

SPORTING SKILLS SERIES

The All-Rounder

PETER WALKER

PELHAM BOOKS

To Sarah, Justin and Daniel,
three top-class all-rounders

First published in Great Britain by
PELHAM BOOKS LTD
52 Bedford Square
London WC1B 3EF
1979

*Photograph on page 92 by Central Press Photos Ltd; all other
photographs by Patrick Eagar*

ISBN 0 7207 1148 7

Phototypeset in Great Britain by
Western Printing Services Ltd, Bristol,
printed by Hollen Street Press, Slough
and bound by Dorstel Press, Harlow

Contents

Introduction

No other player in a team contributes as much to his side's success as the all-rounder. He has twice the number of opportunities to make an impact on a game, and double the work load too. In each of the three main skills, batting, bowling and fielding, he should be regarded as a specialist. (I'm talking here principally about all-round abilities at the highest level, to which every all-rounder with ambition must aspire.) It is often said in selectorial circles that a Test all-rounder should be able to hold his place both as a specialist batsman and a specialist bowler. Now these are high ideals, so high that at the very pinnacle of their careers this claim can only barely be made for such world-class performers as Trevor Bailey, Keith Miller, Ray Illingworth, Richie Benaud, Eddie Barlow, Tony Greig, and even the modern-day Hercules, Ian Botham. Only Gary Sobers in post-war cricket could fully measure up to this yardstick. Even so, the point is well taken.

The comparison between Hercules and the all-rounder in cricket is not without substance. The wear and tear is so much greater than on, say, the opening batsman, who – like the fast bowler – usually spends a fair bit of the match with his feet up watching the others struggle. The all-rounder is usually at the centre of the action, particularly if he bats in the middle order. With the tremendous growth of limited-over cricket in the past fifteen years, middle-order batting has to combine the obduracy of a Bailey if quick wickets have fallen with the explosive scientific slogging of a Botham when 40 are wanted in three overs! Such skills are rare.

From a bowling point of view, the majority of Test all-rounders have been medium-pace or above seam bowlers simply because, of all the arts, this is both the easiest to master and the least tiring. But even here there are extra pressures. In limited-over cricket, medium-pacers are the ones to whom the other members of the team look for a spell of tight containment, but because of their speed they are also the most vulnerable to being taken apart by a hard-hitting, adventurous batsman. Consequently the pressure and responsibilities are redoubled for the all-rounder, both as a batsman and bowler.

The ideal composition of a team is five specialist batsmen, four front-line bowlers, a wicketkeeper and an all-rounder. It follows that although the one all-rounder in the side is going to see a tremendous amount of the action, his opportunities both for selection and for retaining his place against outside competition are limited and wholly dependent on his consistency.

What I've attempted to do in this book is to look at the basic techniques of the game. Let no one sneer at the fundamentals. Tom Graveney, one of the finest stroke-players England has ever produced, had a net, where possible, every day of his professional life. He said he needed the fifteen-minute daily warm-up to check that his technique and coordination were synchronized

Most readers will have been playing the game, perhaps for years, with a variable amount of success. For them I hope that reading this book will suggest a new way of approaching a current difficulty, or provide recognition and thereby a cure for a recurring error. The emphasis throughout will be on the role of the all-rounder in modern cricket and in particular the way that successful cricketers think about the game. But because cricket divides into the separate components of batting, bowling and fielding, it's necessary to look at each in some detail before welding them together into, hopefully, a winning streak.

One thing I will say as a former all-rounder myself: you'll never be bored!

1 To Begin at the Beginning

Obviously any side capable of scoring 400 runs, or in limited-over terms averaging around four runs per over, is going to win more games than it loses! It follows then that a side of eleven reputable batsmen each capable of making 40 has a fair chance of going through a season winning or drawing more often than it loses. Therefore, before any tactical plan can be formulated, your team has to get a reasonable total to which you, as a key member of the middle order, will naturally enough be expected to make a telling contribution in accordance with the state of the game.

A correct batting technique is without doubt the most important basic requirement for the budding all-rounder. If you happen to be an embryonic Bradman or Gower then you can rest assured you'll have precious little opportunity to practise your bowling! Such talent is rare, and it therefore tends to channel itself into just one aspect of the game. But a middle-order batsman arriving at the wicket must have a sound enough method to be able to handle anything from a spin bowler, who has already found his length and confidence through a quick wicket or two, to a fast bowler with the second new ball in his hand. If quick runs are needed, the all-rounder will have next to no time to have a look at the bowling and the pitch or to play himself in – those are the benefits of being an upper-order batsman. So a secure technique is vital. The better technician you are, the more consistent you are bound to be.

A current misconception is to equate consistency with stodginess, but the equation is far from the truth. Consistency means the regular application of your talents and skill to the best of your ability. Only when you have achieved true consistency can your contribution to a winning team become more than the odd flash in the pan.

First let's look at a few basic formulae which in my experience, and that of most other first-class cricketers, create the best framework on which to expand your batting skills. In some respects, golf and cricket have much in common, and it is hardly a coincidence that so many first-class cricketers are also fine golfers. The principles of using a cricket bat or a golf club are well-nigh identical – correct grip and stance, head still, watch the ball.

As in most ball games, the best way is invariably the simplest and most logical. When you look around the club cricket scene, some of the contortions indulged in may hardly qualify for either category, but then much of the game's wealth of humour would disappear if everyone were to become a carbon copy of the MCC coaching manual. Still, apart from some very minor differences, there are several basic requirements which are common to all the best players.

GRIP

The best way of ensuring that you're holding the bat correctly is to lay it face-down in front of you on the ground, then bend down and pick it up just as if you were about to lift it high above your head before chopping a block of wood. This is the correct grip. All you must make sure of is that your hands are close together and positioned towards the top end of the handle.

The reasons for this? The two hands should work as a single unit. Have you ever seen a top-class golfer with his hands far apart on the club shaft? Of course not. For maximum effect the hands should be one unified power centre. And as for being near the top of the handle, it's a matter of pure physics. The longer the arc of the swing of the bat, the faster the hitting face will travel. If you place your hands down near the splice you are in effect 'choking'

A good example of how a
high pair of hands on the
handle enables more wrist
work and power to be
employed. Compare Glenn
Turner's stroke with that
of Eric Russell in the next
picture. Russell's stroke is
identical, but he has
pushed the ball away to
the on side; Glenn Turner
has hit it hard

OPPOSITE *Eric Russell's
hands are low on the bat,
restricting power because
of abbreviated bat swing*

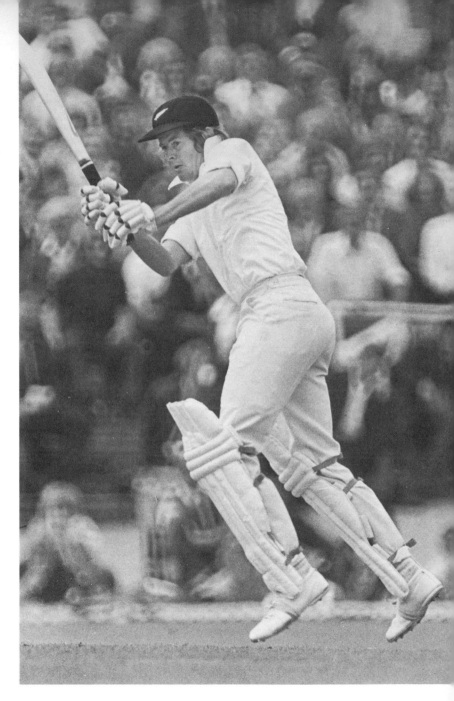

10

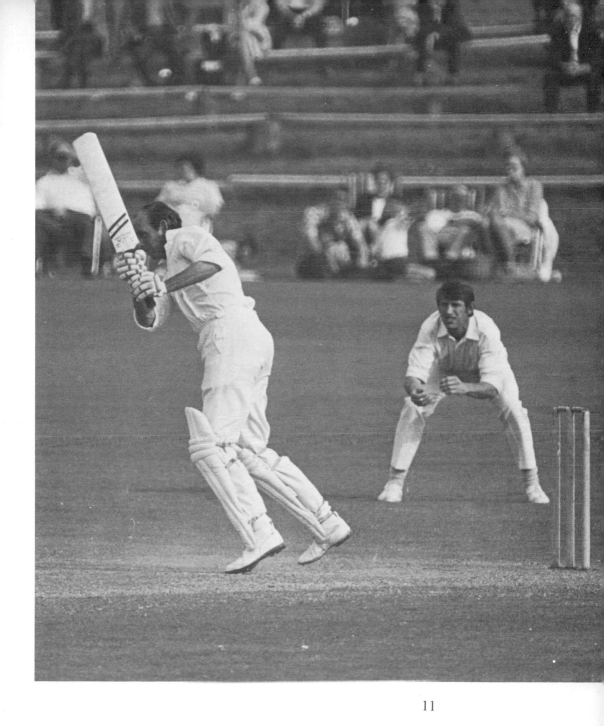

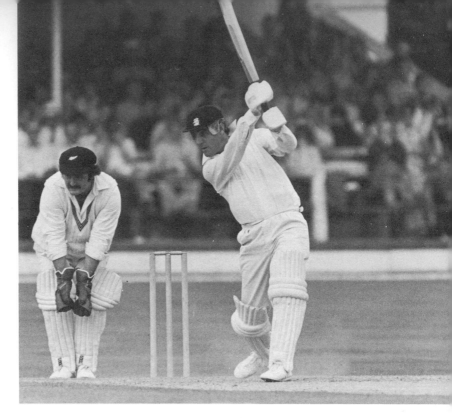

the backswing and thus reducing the amount of force you can exert. A good visual check is to place the bat behind your back foot in your normal stance, then look down. The 'V's' formed between each thumb and forefinger should point somewhere between the outside edge of the bat and the splice. Next time you get near to a top-class batsman, either in the nets or practising on the outfield, look at his grip, for in his hands lies the key to his success.

As to picking the bat up straight – well, I can think of countless first-class batsmen who don't do that, but most of them *come down* straight, and that's what is important. One useful tip if you're worried that you might not be playing as straight as you'd like: in the nets concentrate on keeping the right elbow fairly close to your side as you pick up the bat. Don't lock it in, but on the other hand don't allow your elbow to fly away from your body. That will help, I'm sure.

12

STANCE

Although your grip is now right, you're in no position to maximize this promising beginning unless your body and feet are correctly placed. Whether you're batting, bowling or throwing, cricket is basically a sideways game, so when you take up your stance try to position your body so that it is facing approximately towards point, at 90 degrees to the oncoming bowler. Now I know there are a lot of so-called 'two-eyed' first-class batters. But standing sideways does not prevent you from using both your eyes, unless your neck muscles have been set in concrete! The feet should be

The purist would say that the top hand is a bit too far around towards the back of the bat, but apart from this very minor point Zaheer Abbas here shows a classically comfortable yet alert stance

Barry Richards demonstrates a classically straight pick-up with head and body ideally positioned

roughly parallel with the crease, and as far apart as feels comfortable, bearing in mind that you will have to make a swift decision whether or not to play forward or back. This means that your weight distribution ideally should be about equal on each foot.

Nearly everyone is either a natural front-foot or a natural back-foot player. Sobers often stepped back as his first movement in order to launch himself forward. No one can coach you in this, it's an inherent instinct. You'll soon learn which you prefer, and

14

this in turn will determine your weight distribution. If you're primarily a front-foot batsman then obviously sixty per cent of your weight will be on your back foot, and the reverse applies if you're happier playing back. Because it's harder to play the ball on the leg side, many first-class batsmen pull their front foot slightly back towards the leg side in their stance. They then find it easier to 'open out' to balls pitched on the leg without losing the ability to stretch across to a ball pitched outside the off stump.

Viv Richards – straight pick-up, left side leading, front foot to the pitch of the ball

15

Next time you get out bowled, lbw or caught behind the wicket, ask yourself, 'exactly where did the ball pitch?' It's ten to one that you won't be able to say within the nearest six inches. Not watching the ball is the failing of the great and the not so great, and it's almost impossible to coach someone to do it. It's part and parcel of having 'ball sense', that indefinable attribute that some people have and others haven't. So the advice I can offer is limited, but still worthwhile. When the bowler is running up, for heaven's sake keep your head still! (If you were trying to read a book, for example, you wouldn't bob up and down – your eyes just couldn't focus on the print.) You must give your eyes a chance to pick up the flight and speed of the ball as it leaves the bowler's hand, and they can do that best if they have as few complications as possible set in front of them. Look at someone like David Gower or Geoff Boycott, Barry or Viv Richards. Their heads are rock-still as the bowler approaches. Remember, if a really fast bowler is letting one go at you, you have approximately one fifth of a second in which to judge where the ball is going to pitch and make contact. Don't make things any more difficult by wagging your head around; cricket's a hard enough game to master as it is!

Whatever else you may disbelieve, believe this. You hit the ball with your eyes! Not in a literal sense of course, but it's undoubtedly true that most batsmen are dismissed by their own visual miscalculations rather than being defeated by the bowler. So give your eyes the unconditional freedom to decide whether to play the ball or not, to go forward or back, to attack or defend. If your technique is sound, most of the time they'll be right. After all, without direction from the eyes your limbs can't function.

Besides keeping your head as still as possible, it's also important from your eyes' point of view that you do not allow it to stray away from the oncoming line of the ball. With most deliveries, if you try to let the ball pass through the imaginary line from under your chin straight down to the ground, then this makes it much easier to swing the bat in the pendulum arc which enhances your chances of striking it correctly.

There's an old Aussie saying, 'You can't make any more runs when you're back in the pavilion', and it would not be untrue to say that a fair measure of any first-class batsman's success stems from a selfish love of occupying the crease. Geoff Boycott is contemporary cricket's classic example. Now while I wouldn't suggest that this is a healthy attitude for the amateur player, as an approach to making runs it has few equals.

It takes on average about two and a half to three hours to reach 100. In most cases the first 50 takes longer than the second, for the obvious reasons of having to play oneself in, and often not getting the majority of the strike, etc. Within this time scale the fielding side are likely to bowl in the region of 350 balls, probably 50 of which have real wicket-taking potential. Obviously the higher the grade of cricket, the higher the percentage of dangerous deliveries one is likely to receive. The first problem therefore is to have a good enough defence to keep out these killers. So although it might be like starting a banquet with a glass of flat beer, to occupy the crease for three hours you must be well equipped defensively.

FORWARD DEFENSIVE

The bread-and-butter stroke of batting. As an all-rounder you'll be needing this stroke more than most if your side is struggling to stave off defeat, with only a wicket or two in hand and fielders crowding around the bat!

The art is to drop the ball as near to your own feet as possible. The things to concentrate on are these. Get your front foot as far out and as near to where the ball pitches as possible. But never overstretch so that the front leg is locked, because there must be flexibility in the knee to help stun the ball. The head must be kept well over the ball. The bat should pass very close to the front pad, and should be at an angle of around 45° when it makes contact with the ball alongside the leading knee. The other point to watch is that the grip should not be too tight – a firm push will cause an edged ball to fly at catchable height to the close fielders. The top

Geoff Boycott's bat and front pad are close together, leaving no gap through which the ball may pass. His left hand is dominant, he has a good sideways position, his head is still and his eyes are on the ball. His bat is virtually stationary and his hands are ahead of the face of the blade

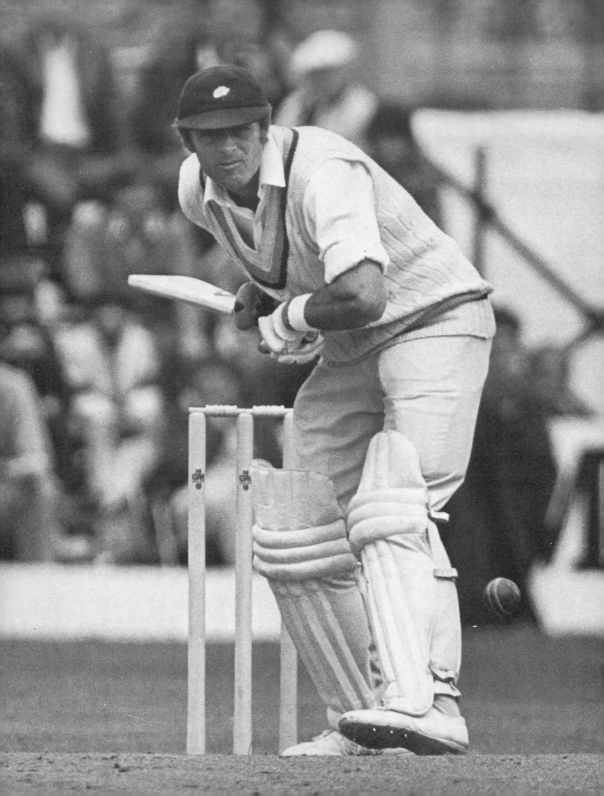

hand should always be in control – indeed the other probably does no more than to rest thumb and forefinger round the bat handle.

The finest exponent of this block – it would be an exaggeration to call it a stroke or shot – was Trevor Bailey, the Essex and England all-rounder. He perfected it to such a degree that his defence became well-nigh impregnable, and the nickname of 'Barnacle' stuck like the proverbial limpet! It needs a great deal of concentration and muscle control to master the forward defensive push, but every batsman in history who has made an impact in Wisden has had it in his repertoire.

BACK DEFENSIVE

Here the most important thing to aim for is to make sure that you have stepped back and across in front of your stumps. This will enable you to (a) protect your wicket and (b) decide whether the ball needs to be played at all.

Watch a great batsman start an innings. It's not the number of balls that he plays that should impress you, it's the number he leaves alone! Similar principles to the forward defensive apply when playing back, particularly those of keeping sideways-on.

Whenever you start a practice session in the nets, my suggestion is that you first work at perfecting your defensive techniques.

Now to the more positive side – scoring runs. There are not many batsmen who hit the ball equally hard off the front and back foot. Viv Richards is one who immediately springs to mind, but then he is a batting genius. You have to decide which is your forte and then wait for the right delivery to come along to bring it into play.

Most of the strong drivers of the ball on the front foot give themselves a little room to hit it. By this I mean that they do not get their leading leg right to the pitch of the ball – a first requirement in defensive play. Ian Botham, the England all-rounder, who hits the ball as hard as any contemporary player off the front

21

22

foot, is a good example of this. Giving oneself room in effect increases the leverage and permits a freer swing of the blade. So if you're trying to give the ball a mighty whack off the front foot, don't worry about it not being absolutely classically straight.

The key here is not to try to hit the ball too hard and not to take your eye off the ball as you strive for maximum effort. Unless you're in a situation which demands desperate measures, a broad rule of thumb is not to hit across the ball. In other words, if it pitches outside the off stump, hit it out on the off side. A helpful tip here is that the ball will usually go in the direction that your bat starts in its follow-through. But of course all sorts of other factors can modify this – the state of the wicket, the placing of the field and the angle of the oncoming ball. We'll come to this later when we discuss tactics and attitudes.

As in all things in cricket, the head is the centre of gravity. Keep it as still and as upright as possible and this will help you retain your balance, particularly during those difficult on-side strokes where there is a tendency to fall over oneself.

The back-foot attacking strokes are more varied, but in all bar one case the importance of keeping sideways-on to allow the bat a full, free swing cannot be over-emphasized. That exception is the hook shot. Here speed of foot and a square-on position to the bowler are essential requirements. The thing to make sure of is to roll the wrists over the ball on impact, otherwise there's a strong chance of hitting it in the air. Most of the great hookers have been short men – Washbrook, Bradman, Bill Edrich, Fredericks – so my advice to you if you're over six feet tall is beware the hook: although it's a stroke that brings a lot of runs, because you've only got what amounts to the bat's width of $4\frac{1}{4}$ inches in which to strike the ball, the room for error is enormous. If however you can play it, and play it well, it's a demoralizing slap in the ego for the bowler, particularly if he thinks he's quick!

Now, having absorbed the above and hopefully practised enough for it all to have become second nature, how do you put it all together out in the middle? As an all-rounder, let's assume that your arrival at the wicket follows a good if somewhat steady start

Gordon Greenidge, one of
the world's greatest
hookers – back in front of
his stumps, terrific body
thrust, eyes on the ball

by the team's specialist batsmen, but that the scoring rate will soon have to be stepped up.

Batting can be said to fall into three stages, rather like a bullfight. In the opening stanza, the bull, or bowler, is fresh, eager for the kill and throws everything into the attack. Once the matador/batsman has survived this initial onslaught and blunted the bull's speed, the scene changes to act two, where the bull, still full of fight but with a new respect for his adversary, begins to wonder just how he is going to trap his opponent. Act three is the domination of the bull by the matador, the bowler by the batsman.

Even here danger lurks. Just as the bull may produce a sudden toss of the head, so too might a bowler spring a surprise on an over-confident batsman. So vigilance, or to put it another way, concentration, is of vital importance throughout for both bull-fighter and batsman.

What should be going through your mind as you walk out to bat? Remembering Oscar Wilde, that 'the best thing to do with good advice is to pass it on to someone else, for one rarely uses it oneself', I would suggest but three little words: 'Watch the ball, watch the ball, watch the ball.' Forget everything else. This is just another way of saying 'concentrate'.

How does one define concentration? Not easily, but I would say that it is the ability to exclude all premeditated thought from your conscious state. Remember my earlier advice to play the ball with your eyes? This means that you should shut out all thoughts about a bowler's reputation, the state of the wicket, the form you're in and, initially, the target your side has set itself. Concentration should mean standing there relaxed but ready, the mind clear of any deflecting thoughts except the phrase, 'watch the ball'. In time this will become habit, and certainly as your innings grows in both length and stature the need for such simplicity becomes less keen and one can begin to look objectively at the field, searching for likely gaps. In other words, concentration is NOT premeditated movement, or a thinking out of all the possibilities open. It is a scrutiny of the bowler's action in releasing the ball and its subsequent flight to the exclusion of all other thoughts, leaving the technical side to take care of itself. This principle applies to batting, bowling and fielding.

Once you've taken guard and looked around at the fielding positions, besides survival your most pressing anxiety is getting the first run. All batsmen have a deep fear of making 0. In first-class cricket the greatest pressure by a fielding side is always exerted at this point. Psychologically it's the most important run of an innings. So don't try to hit the skin off the first half-volley that comes along. Always play well within yourself when you first go in. That doesn't mean to say that you should be slack or unassertive. Just realize that the firm controlled push for one or two runs is a safer bet than a full-blooded drive during your first twenty minutes or so at the crease. This is known in the trade as 'building an innings'.

Ray Lindwall, that superb Australian fast bowler and astute assessor of opposing batsmen, once said, 'The best place to get runs when you first come in is at the backing-up end!' Ray knew what he was talking about. It's far easier to absorb the general atmosphere of the game, the pace of the pitch, the speed of the bowler, the 'feel' of the game, without the responsibility of actually having to play the ball. Sir Len Hutton was a pastmaster of keeping away from the danger end early in an innings; not that he wasn't a good enough player, he just liked to have enough time to weigh things up at his own tempo.

Successful batting is all about developing good habits. One tip when you first go in is not to talk too much to either the opposition, your batting partner or the umpires. Remember that 'cocoon of concentration'. Look inward at the start, minimize the possibility of error, and your career will blossom.

All the finest players have good habits. When they first come in they attempt very little by way of positive scoring strokes – always providing time isn't against them. They also tend to play the ball straight back in a 'V' between mid-off and mid-on, and never play across the line of flight.

Having survived the early thunderbolts, your innings now

moves into its second act. With your eye in, and having perhaps ridden a bit of early luck when you've played and missed without getting an edge, or even been dropped by a fielder, you're now accepted by the opposition as a fixture at the crease with a high nuisance factor. You'll probably find that the odd attacking fielder has been withdrawn, and this in itself will do wonders for your batting morale. It's now that you should start to make yourself felt on the scoresheet. This period of transition usually lasts around half an hour, or 15 or so runs.

Once you reach 30, a watershed at all levels of cricket, the action shifts into phase three. It is here where your skills should take control of the situation. In a sense the fielding side now take their lead from you. Depending on your degree of aggression they will react with bowling changes and increasingly negative field placings. From this point on, the termination of your innings should be of your own making, either through a miscalculation on your part or from sheer fatigue.

What I've been describing is the method employed by all the world's finest batsmen in building an innings. Their high scores and consistency do not rely purely on natural flair. There is method – and consistently similar method at that – in their approach to the problems of starting an innings.

Tony Greig lost in a cocoon of concentration during a Test match

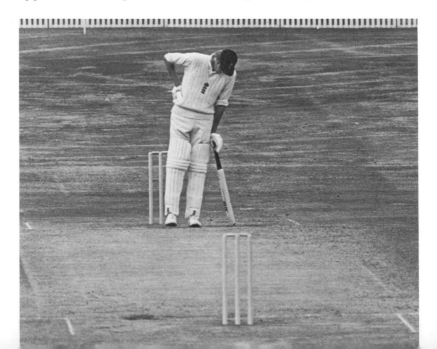

The all-rounder will more often than not have less time available to put all this into practice. Nevertheless the principles, if not the speed of execution, remain the same. To keep the score ticking along, the ability to push the ball gently towards a fielder stationed some twenty yards from the bat and then scamper a single with an alert partner is one of the best and certainly most effective ways of both keeping the score moving and disrupting your opponents' plans. The secret here is not to hit the ball too hard and only to run if the fielder is very deep or if you've hit the ball to his non-throwing side. It's surprising how quickly you will weigh up the fielders . . . this is information you can store away while at the backing-up end.

What then are the main differences between a Test batsman and the talented club player? I think they are worth recording, not so much as a detrimental comparison but rather to show how a Test player reaches the top.

The biggest gap lies between their levels of application. The club batsman, having successfully survived the crucial opening twenty minutes of his innings, begins to believe that he's Wally Hammond reincarnate. Suddenly a delicate late cut ends sadly in the safe hands of the wicketkeeper – out for a well-played 15! Even allowing for the longer time scale, the Test player on the other hand has an instinctive feel about his own prowess and current form. Even when not quite in touch, he'll still get runs, because he concentrates on achieving all the basics we've already covered. The first-class batsman regards every ball as a fresh challenge, and has the gift of being able to wipe clean the slate of memory concerning the previous delivery. Also, good players rarely go to the wicket without believing they're going to make a big score. It may sound arrogant, but no class player is without this inner high opinion of himself. He knows he has the talent, is confident in his basic technique, and has a history of success behind him.

Getting one's first hundred is like trying to run a four-minute mile – once done, it's a lot easier. So set yourself various targets . . . 30 runs to start with, then go up in tens until a century's in sight.

2 The Other Side of the Coin

Having made your contribution with the bat, now comes the time to field. All-rounders are lucky here, because once again they'll be right in the middle of the action. Sometimes, if you're the team's Ian Botham, you'll be expected to take the new ball a matter of just ten minutes after coming off the field with perhaps a long tiring innings under your belt.

It's not easy to switch from the type of concentration needed for batting to that required for bowling – and they are very different in many respects. The phrase 'a thoughtful bowler' is often used these days when critics are commenting on performers like Phil Edmunds (almost in the Test all-rounder class), Chris Old and Mike Hendrick. What do they mean? Well, much of the preparation for the next ball is done while you're walking back to your mark. Unlike batting, where it's best to clear your mind and concentrate on one ball at a time, bowlers must have a variety of permutations running through their heads all the time they're bowling. A lot also depends on what kind of bowler you are and how many arrows you have in your quiver – i.e. the different number of types of delivery you have at your command.

All the great bowlers have had what amounts to an encyclopedic memory of batsmen they've played against and how they got them out. It's also important, particularly in games when you're coming up against unknown opposition, to be able to quickly analyse a batsman's strengths and weaknesses. This could mean that he'll hit you for a few runs before the message has sunk in, but once you've discovered, say, that he's suspect outside the off stump but very strong on his legs, don't ever bowl him

OPPOSITE *Even someone like Dennis Lillee, who relies on explosive power, needs to out-think a batsman*

another ball that pitches any further towards the leg side than middle stump!

Another thing. Although you're obviously hopeful of getting a man out every ball, only the foolish optimist or the tearaway fast bowler – they're often one and the same human being – really expects to strike every time. It's best to plan your campaign with a specific mode of eventual dismissal in mind. The finest bowler of this type I've ever come across was Tommy Cartwright, the former England, Warwickshire, Somerset and Glamorgan medium-pacer. Tommy used to call it 'pattern bowling'. By this he meant that he would nag away at a batsman, bowling him say a succession of awayswingers, encouraging him to drive on the front foot. Then, perhaps ten balls later, Tommy would slip in the inswinger to trap him lbw or even bowl a man who had got so used to playing at him in one way that the change of direction completely nonplussed him. Of course accurate bowling like this not only needs great concentration – because in a medium-pace or spin bowler's world a spell can last two hours or more – it also requires a tremendous amount of practice.

Because this book is intended for all-rounders, let's have a brief look at various types of bowling; yours is bound to be amongst them. In all cases the two 'L's' are obligatory: without line and length you'll never truly succeed, even if you can bowl it as fast as Bob Willis or as subtly as Phil Edmonds. I'm afraid line and length aren't handed down genetically. They're achieved only after hours and hours of concentrated net practice. No one, not even that inspired cricketing genius Gary Sobers, was exempt from the chore of bowling practice in the nets.

It might be as well at this point to define length and line. The ideal length is the spot on the pitch which creates uncertainty in the batsman's mind about whether to play forward or back. Line is best described by visualizing three imaginary straight lines drawn between the stumps at each end. Normally a right-handed bowler delivering from over the wicket would aim to pitch the ball just outside the batsman's off-stump line. Providing the ball does not either swing in the air or spin after pitching, the angle from which the bowler has let the ball go should mean that it will hit the off or middle stump.

Let's now look at the different types of bowling. As an all-rounder it's unlikely that you'll be a genuine fast bowler, because of the effort needed, but just in case, here goes.

FAST BOWLING

At the outset, let me say that it is impossible to coach somebody to bowl genuinely fast. Either you can or you can't, it's as simple and as straightforward as that. Fast bowling combines brute strength, suppleness, rhythm and timing – you have to have a measure of each. Some people can only bowl fast: Frank Tyson found and Wayne Daniels now finds it nearly impossible to release the ball slowly and still retain a measure of control.

Assuming you do have natural pace, how do you best exploit it? It is pointless charging in from a twenty-five-yard run to fire the ball with the speed of light three feet either side of the batsman. You should aim to make him play every ball. Unlike the medium-pacer, you're not trying to outwait your opponent. Like a meteor, you burn brightly but die quickly, so for heaven's sake make the batsman play. Unless you do so it will be a criminal waste of the hard shiny new ball, which always bounces a little higher than an old one, a factor which doubles the problems of survival for the batsman. Nothing is more infuriating to a fielding captain or more relieving to a shaky batsman than to be able to let the ball fly harmlessly by without having to offer a shot.

Try to pitch the ball on its raised seam. This will give it a chance to deviate off the wicket. To do this, always hold the ball with the seam facing the batsman, and do not roll the wrist on delivery to either the left or right. A loose supple wrist with a firm but not too tight grip is essential. If you rotate your wrist at the point of release, a lot of the forward force will be lost, and remember that as a fast bowler you're trying to get the ball down to the other end as quickly as possible.

Measure out a run-up which lets you arrive at the crease on balance, in control of your movements, yet moving fast enough to provide the 'whip' so necessary in pace bowling. Also, try to get as close to the wicket as possible at the moment of delivery. This will help you get a good body turn, which takes some of the effort out of bowling quick. If you're a right-hander you should start your delivery stride with your left shoulder pointing at the batsman and finish with a 180° turn, so that your right shoulder now faces him.

The higher you can stretch your leading arm, the faster you are likely to be able to bowl, because this movement braces the left side and gives you the necessary resistance to rotate against. The whole of your left side, and in particular your braced front leg, should provide a firm yet flexible fulcrum for the action. At release try to keep your bowling arm as high as comfortably possible. I know that a lot of fast bowlers, Ray Lindwall in particular, had seemingly lowish arms. But photographic examination reveals that they have let their bodies fall away towards the off side, making it look as if the action is a trifle round-arm. In fact, all good quickies have a well-nigh vertical delivery arm position at release – this is what gives them that awkward bounce off the wicket.

As a fast bowler, never, never overpitch. Many coaching manuals will tell you to bowl a full length, but no fast bowler worthy of the name enjoys being driven off the front foot. Your length should be around the mark which causes the batsman a feeling of physical uncertainty. Please don't read this as a recipe for a barrage of bouncers. Recent concern about short-pitched deliveries at Test match level has brought a somewhat feeble attempt from Lords to protect the tail-end batsman less able to fend for himself. The first Packer series in Australia saw thirteen men hit on the head, mainly by the phalanx of West Indian fast bowlers, Holding, Roberts, Daniel, Garner and Croft, who must have got perilously close to a charge of assault and battery. The cricketing crash helmet was born during this series, and one American watching a Packer night game was heard to say, 'Boy, this is the greatest blood sport in the world!'

34

The start of Michael
Holding's twenty-yard
run-up: perfectly balanced,
and without any evidence
of strain

In full flight,
approximately eight to ten
yards before delivery. Note
how still Holding keeps
his head, his eyes
searching out the target
area on the pitch

The pre-delivery stride. The body is in the process of turning to a fully sideways-on position; the leading arm is about to reach skywards to extend the whole left side; the seam of the ball is vertical

CENTRE *The explosive power at release. The left arm is pulling down and past the braced left hip and leg, the right arm is high, the wrist vertical, the eyes still on the target area*

FAR RIGHT *The follow-through: the right shoulder is swinging round to finish pointing at the batsman, the wrist is straight – there is no sideways spin imparted to the ball; the head is steady, the eyes are looking at the target area*

LEFT *Dennis Lillee's pre-delivery stride. The left shoulder is swinging around to point at the batsman, taking with it the left hip. By the time the right foot is grounded, Lillee's whole body will be sideways-on to the batsman*

ABOVE *Bob Willis's delivery stride. The left arm is pulling down past the left hip to allow the right arm to accelerate through without interference*

Bob Willis bowls a
bouncer to Shafiq Ahmad
of Pakistan — the ball is
straight and not too high,
forcing the batsman to
think about playing at it

Fast bowling, if it means anything at all, is about letting the ball go with aggression. Bob Willis was rightly condemned for his round-the-wicket bouncer at a Pakistani tail-ender in the 1978 series in England, when Iqbal Qasim needed medical attention after being hit in the mouth in the first Test at Edgbaston. All the same, a bouncer always has been and always should be part of a fast bowler's armament. If you bowl it short, it must be directed at the batsman to have any effect, otherwise it has as much wicket-taking potential as a wet marshmallow. A cricket ball is a very hard, potentially lethal weapon, so use the bouncer sparingly. Not to bowl it at all means that out on the field you may be too nice a guy to make a top-class fast bowler.

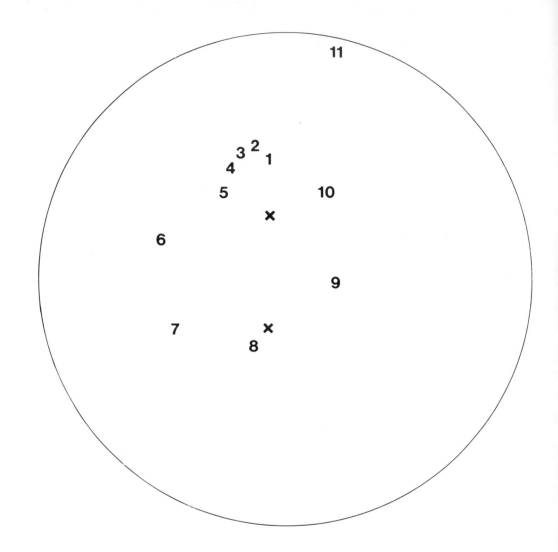

Attacking field, fast or medium-fast bowler, mainly away swingers: 1 wicketkeeper, 2 1st slip, 3 2nd slip, 4 3rd slip, 5 gulley, 6 cover, 7 squarish mid-off, 8 bowler, 9 straightish mid-wicket, 10 backward short leg, 11 deep fine leg

Notes: *the slips are staggered in depth with at least a full arm's stretch between them. If the ball is swinging a lot, 10 can move over to either 4th slip or second gulley*

44

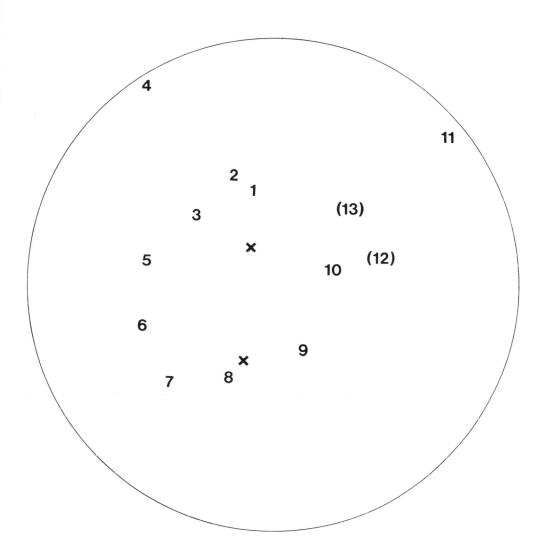

Defensive field, fast or medium-fast bowling. Not swinging, aiming on or outside the off stump:
1 wicketkeeper, 2 1st slip, 3 gulley, 4 third man, 5 cover point, 6 extra cover, 7 mid-off, 8 bowler, 9 mid-on, 10 mid-wicket, 11 deep square leg/long leg

Notes: If the attack is being slanted towards the leg side, gulley moves to a position near square leg umpire (12), 4 moves squarer on the boundary, 7 can either join 9 and 10 in the leg side arc or else go to the deep position saving the one, (13), with 11 moving finer

MEDIUM-PACE BOWLING

The bulk of the work load in any side falls on the medium-pacer. All the basic principles already covered in the action apply, as they do in all forms of bowling. Remember, it's a sideways game. But because the medium-paced bowler is that much slower, he needs more accuracy and greater control than the genuine 'quickie'. A lot of attention should be paid to the way you grip the ball.

I suppose the most successful medium-pacer around at the moment is the Somerset all-rounder, Ian Botham. His Test record is phenomenal, yet a mere two years ago he was just another change bowler for his county. Why has he come on so? Certainly he has the innate skill, but he also works at his bowling.

Ian is one of those rare birds that can swing the ball either way at will. He can also do this with precious little change in his action, which would give the game away to an observant batsman. First of all he holds the ball firmly but not too tightly, with his thumb resting passively alongside the seam. Depending on whether he wants to bowl an inswinger or an outswinger, he slightly angles the direction that the seam of the ball is facing towards the direction he wants it to swing. Lastly, he places the shiny side of the ball on the leg side if he wants to make the ball swing away towards the slips, and on the off side if he wants it to go towards the batsman's pads from outside the off stump. Aerodynamically the reasoning is obvious. The shiny side of a round object will travel through the air faster than the non-polished side because there is less drag. This is why you'll note that a first-class swing bowler only polishes one side of the ball.

Ian then runs up and attempts to deliver both the awayswinger and the inswinger with as near an identical high arm action as he can. For the awayswinger he slightly pushes the little finger side of his hand through first, for the inswinger the thumb side. But all the time he makes sure that the ball leaves his hand with the seam vertical, so that when it arives at the other end it pitches on it.

Given a reasonably shiny ball, most bowlers have the ability to

46

swing the ball one way. But to be a top-class bowler of this kind you must be able to do both. And that means practice! To make the ball swing away from the bat, get as close to the stumps as possible at delivery, thereby assisting the drift of direction towards the slips. For the inswinger, a position at the edge of the delivery or return crease has a similar helpful effect. But obviously if you do this each time your body placement will give the game away, so practise trying to bowl both kinds from the same position on the crease.

What makes a ball swing late in its flight? I've never met anyone who has successfully explained why. Some people, like Botham, have the inborn ability to get the ball to alter course only a few feet in front of the batsmen; others swing it like a banana all the way from the hand. Obviously the later the ball swings, the harder it is for the batsman to play.

The difference between swing and seam bowling again cannot be explained scientifically. Bob Willis does not swing the ball much, yet often produces what amount to fast off-breaks off the pitch. Mike Hendrick and Chris Old don't swing the ball a great deal either, but in favourable conditions they move it prodigiously off the seam.

Seam bowling is a bit of a hit-or-miss business. Even the finest bowlers of this type cannot nominate with any certainty which way they're going to move it, but what they have in common with all bowlers is that they strive to pitch the ball on the seam. However, more than any other type of bowler they bang it into the wicket to achieve maximum affect.

Max Walker, close to the wickets to aid his movement away from the bat and off the pitch. Note the angle of the seam

SPIN BOWLING

Off-spinners flourish more in the United Kingdom than abroad, where they're considered a nondescript species rather than the matchwinners they can be. In recent times only Tayfield of South Africa, Gibbs of the West Indies and Prasanna of India have been fit to rate with several English off-spinners of whom Jim Laker was the supreme artist.

Few spinners agree completely on the type of grip to use. We're in the world of individual skill here, not the explosive force used by faster bowlers. But all spinners would go along with the theory that once again the ball should *land* on the seam to give it maximum purchase and grip. Occasionally one should try not to pitch it thus, in order to make the ball 'skid' through, but in general spinners also conform to basic principles. The slower you bowl, the more likely is the ball to turn, as it is in contact with the ground that fraction of a second longer. As well as that, the steeper the angle of descent the more the spin will bite. Of course, the slower the speed the more accurate you have to be, for a fleet-footed batsman can make mincemeat of what would otherwise be a good-length ball.

Like quality wines, spin bowlers often take years to mature, but because of its greater variety theirs is one of the most satisfying aspects of the game to master. Fierce concentration is needed to bowl over after over of precision-length spin, and to deceive a batsman, particularly with a small change in the flight of the ball, is one of the game's most rewarding experiences.

All things start with your grip on the ball, and although there is a standard method, don't be afraid to experiment to find out what suits you best and brings the most impressive results. The first difference between yourself and the faster bowlers is that you don't hold the ball with the seam upright, pointing at the batsman. The stitching should be at right-angles to the line of flight. Now place your fingers across the seam. (Don't hold the ball down in the palm of your hand; spin bowling is about touch, so well up into the fingers, please.) Then spread your middle finger and index finger as far apart as feels comfortable, letting the other fingers and thumb fall naturally into place.

The majority of orthodox spinners, both left and right, spin the ball from off their index fingers. Early in the season big spinners of the ball often develop a blister on the inside part of that finger which becomes a hard skin callus as time goes on. The middle joint of Jim Laker's spinning finger is twice as thick as the equivalent on his left hand, as a result of the extra exercise it has received from bowling thousands of overs. The reason for splitting the index and middle fingers as wide apart as possible is that this is

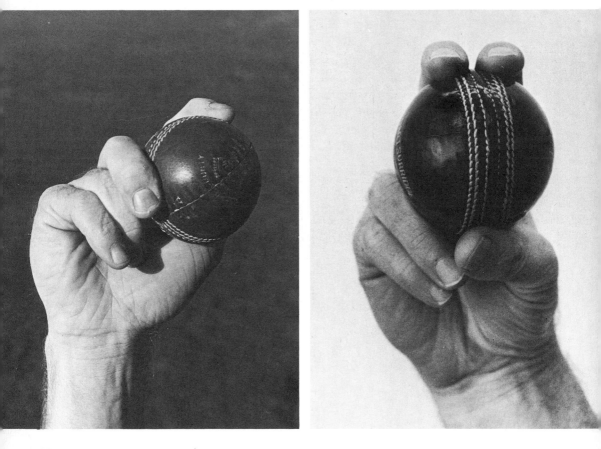

The orthodox grip for the off-spinner. The ball is wedged in between the index and middle fingers. Most of the spin is imparted by the index finger

The grip for the out- or away-spinner. The seam is pointing towards first slip; the shine is on the little-finger side of the ball

the only way to create any real leverage – a fundamental necessity in spinning the ball.

Now a lot of 'spinners' do little more than roll the ball out of the hand, which makes bowling a length and line much easier, although of course unless you're bowling on a very helpful wicket there'll be precious little deviation off the pitch at the other end. Hugh Tayfield was one of this kind, but he was a master at tiny flight variations and had a beautiful arm ball which went slightly towards the slips after pitching. He did this by undercutting the ball at release rather than spinning it.

The inswing grip. The seam is pointing towards leg slip; the shiny side of the ball is on the inside

The orthodox grip for the right-hand leg break and googly. The spin is generated from the index, middle and third fingers. For the googly, the little finger is in contact with the ball last; the wrist is dropped at the point of delivery and the ball actually emerges from the back of the hand

Jim Laker, on the other hand, was the complete off-spinner with his classical sideways action, braced left side and high delivery arm. He spun it a great deal, but also had a tantalizing curved flight which made it extremely difficult to judge exactly where the ball would land.

Most spinners come into one category or the other. The more you spin the ball the harder it is to retain control, particularly over length. Here again practice is the only answer, but don't get discouraged or stop trying to give the ball the maximum amount of tweak you can.

Your line of attack should be just on or outside the off stump, and just as it's a criminal offence for a fast bowler to consistently overpitch, so a spin bowler should chalk it up as a black mark every time a batsman plays back to him . . . that is unless he's misjudged the flight! Batsmen sometimes momentarily lose sight of the ball when playing forward, and a turning delivery will exploit this to the full. Playing back also gives the batsman that precious little bit of extra time in which to see and play the ball. And if you continue to bowl short you also run the risk of losing the lives and certainly the friendship of those team mates who field close in to your bowling!

The off-spin as performed by Ray Illingworth: a good braced left side, the eyes on the spot on the pitch where the ball will land. Note the finger-tip control right up to the moment of release

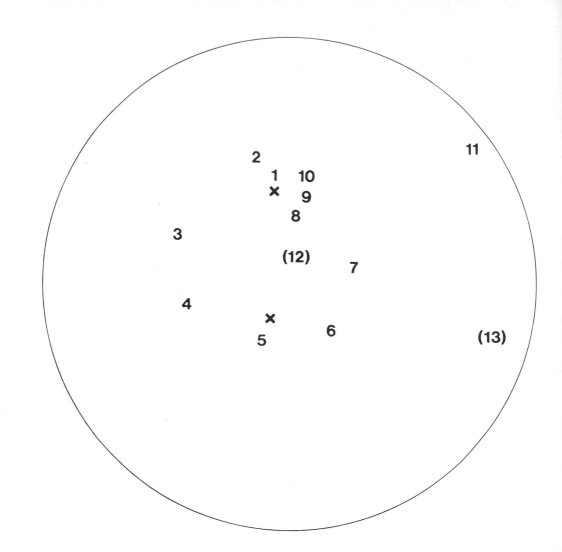

Attacking field, inswing or off-spin bowling:
1 wicketkeeper, 2 1st slip, 3 cover, 4 mid-off, 5 bowler,
6 mid-on, 7 mid-wicket, 8 forward short leg, 9 short
square leg, 10 backward short leg, 11 deep square leg
(fine)

Notes: *If the ball is swinging or turning a lot and the*
batsman starts chancing his arm you can either withdraw 8
to silly mid-on (12) or else post him near the mid-wicket
boundary (13). Alternatively, put 4 into this position, but
then your accuracy must be spot-on not to bowl outside the off
stump, overpitch or drop short, thus giving away a certain
four runs. A slow left-hander will have to move 8, 9 and 10:
they will cross over to gulley, point and extra cover

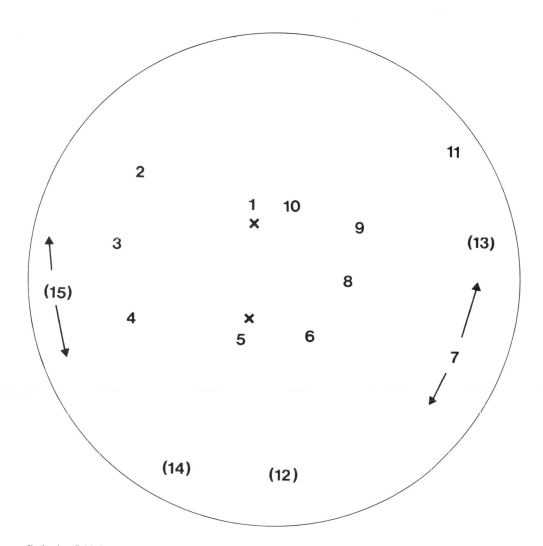

Defensive field, inswing or off-spin bowling:
1 wicketkeeper, 2 short third man, 3 cover, 4 squarish
mid-off, 5 bowler, 6 mid-on (drops back further for
strong driver), 7 deep mid-wicket, 8 mid-wicket,
9 square leg, 10 backward short leg, 11 deep square leg

Notes: 10 can be withdrawn and put back ten yards to
a run-saving position. 11 then moves squarer. Depending
on the batsman's style, the position of 7 will vary, either
towards long-on (12) or squarer (13). A slow
left-hander will have a slip instead of 10; 9 will then
go to (14) and 7 will cross over to the off side to (15)

Leg-spinners are rare: Benaud, Mushtaq and Chandrasekhar are about the only three in post-war times to have lasted any length at the highest level. The sharp inward turn of the wrist at release is a most unnatural action, so the incidence of bad balls is much higher than in the orthodox spinner. Like the little girl with the curl, leg-spinners can be unplayable one day, unforgivably bad the next. So control is the biggest hurdle for a leg-spinner to overcome. The ball is released from a grip which differs from that used by the off-spinner in that the fingers are spread more evenly across the seam and the ball is certainly not held so tightly.

Keeping on balance is essential for this type of bowling, and, initially anyway, do not try to spin it too much. Your line of attack should be on or just outside the off stump, and beware of dropping the ball too short, for even more so than the off-spinner you're wide open to be smashed away through gaps on both the off and leg side.

Leg-break bowlers are a special breed, and here I include the googly too, which is where the right-hander bowls what looks like a leg-break but because the ball comes out of the back of the hand at the point of release it in fact emerges spinning in the opposite direction.

Leg-spinning can be rather like putting: you can go through the fundamental movements, but in the end it's best to adopt the method which suits you best. One thing I can assure you: you'll always be capable of producing the unexpected!

Left-hand bowlers start their season with a twenty-five wicket advantage. Everything is stacked in their favour. Their natural turn, from leg to off, is the hardest type of spin for a right-handed batsman to counter, and if accurately controlled on or outside the off stump it is the most economical form of bowling in the game. In normal circumstances it is harder for a left-hander bowling around the wicket to extract any appreciable turn compared to a right-hander from over the wicket, a factor that isn't often taken into account by coaches. An off-spinner usually bowls over the wicket, except in the case where the ball is turning a lot where, in order to give himself a better chance of hitting the wickets plus an

Phil Edmonds here gives a marvellous illustration of getting into a classically sideways-on position prior to release

The leading right arm is reaching high to provide the pivotal resistance for the left; the head is looking inside the leading arm; the back foot is about to land parallel to the bowling crease

lbw decision, he changes to bowling around; whereas the slow left-hander almost always operates from around the wicket. However, there is a modern trend, begun by Derek Underwood and continued by Phil Edmonds, to switch to over if there is very little turn in the pitch or if there are bowler's rough footmarks to aim for at the other end. The change of angle certainly helps the ball to spin more. With this in mind, on firm pitches the left-hander from around the wicket should aim to land the ball about six inches outside the off stump, so that if it goes straight on it will hit off or middle.

After release: the left shoulder has turned through 180° from its position in the previous plate; the head and eyes are still; the right side is braced

Bowling is a part of the game where natural ability counts for more than almost anything else. But if you bear these few tips in mind and use your own initiative and net facilities to the utmost, you should be well on the way to getting rid of most batsman awaiting you at the other end.

On to more general thoughts about bowling. One of the most appealing things about this aspect of the game is that you've got a chance every ball. A bowler has infinitely more opportunities to succeed than a batsman, and all the great sides of the past – like the Surrey XI in the 1950s, or the West Indies in the 1960s – had tremendous bowling strength in depth. Bowlers, not batsmen, win matches, so let's look at the mental way in which you should approach your task.

The best bowling psychologist in modern cricket was unquestionably Freddie Trueman. He could remember *every* player he bowled at throughout his long career, where he scored most of his runs, and most important of all, where he usually got out. Fred used to take around about 130 wickets a year in county cricket, and by his own reckoning forty per cent of these were because he knew how to 'psych' the batsman out.

If you're a fast bowler, remember that no one actually enjoys facing you. The batsman who boasts on these lines in the dressing room is a hypocrite. The thought of being physically hurt is always in a batsman's mind when he meets a fast bowler, so play on that and attack him. By this I do not literally mean launch into a bouncer war or a lot of bad language. Simply try to make him feel as unwelcome as possible. Killer instinct is vital in the make-up of a fast bowler's temperament. Without it you'll become as hostile as a spent cartridge. In order to increase the batsman's sense of being unwanted, try never to present him with a ball that he can lean forward to and drive. To sustain the pressure – and this in itself is a marvellous wicket-taker – you have to keep after him, making him feel that every time you run up not only his wicket but also his person is in danger.

Change of pace is a prime asset in all kinds of bowling, but the

62

63

fast bowler shouldn't worry about trying to get a lot of variation in speed, because small alterations are far more potent than an obvious 'balloon' of a ball. Most of the best fast bowlers only let one or two balls an over go at maximum speed. It's a wearing business bowling fast, and particularly after a bouncer – which needs a lot of effort – there is sometimes a need to bowl the next one well within yourself. Unless of course you bowl another bumper as a surprise item!

One thing that both medium-pace bowlers and their faster brothers concentrate on is the condition of the ball. Really work on it. Rub it hard down your flannels. Fred Trueman's ample rump made a superb buffer. The smoother and more polished you can keep one side of the ball, the more chance it will have of swinging. The laws prevent you from using anything artificial on the surface as an aid, but this does not include honest sweat. Remember the old army maxim: a combination of spit and polish brings up the brightest, shiniest finish.

One tip. Wear woollen socks as these make a very good polishing agent. Nylon and other man-made fibres are far less effective. If you're a medium-pace bowler and the chap on at the other end is a spinner, keep after him to polish the ball during his over. Spinners tend to forget this because they're more interested in having a rough surface to help their grip. But they can still get this on the 'untreated' side of the ball.

As a bowler you can learn an awful lot by watching a batsman when he's got strike at the other end. From your position in the field, see if he has a pronounced foot movement before your team mate bowls, and if he has, in which direction. When your turn comes to bowl, force the batsman into changing his natural movement. Study the batsman's stance. If he's a right-hander who looks over his left shoulder with left elbow pronouncedly jutting out, it's fairly certain he'll find it difficult to play an inswinger or any delivery pitched on his legs. Similarly, an open-chested batsman is often highly suspect outside the off stump, where he has to lunge at the ball to compensate for his square-on stance.

64

Try changing the angle from which you release the ball. Although in general one should attempt to get as close to the stumps as possible, an occasional six- to nine-inch alteration of your position on the bowling crease will force the batsman into making an adjustment to his stroke, sometimes with fatal consequences. If you swing the ball, varying the position from where you deliver also helps to deceive the batsman into imagining that the ball has swung a great deal, whereas in reality he has been beaten by misjudging the angle.

This is also good advice if you're a spinner. Many first-class off-spinners – for instance John Emburey of Middlesex and England, and Ray Illingworth, the recently retired Leicestershire captain – are very good exponents of this subtlety, and of course the master of them all was Fred Titmus. Fred was not a particularly big spinner of the ball but his use of the crease and the arm ball which drifted away towards the off side brought him countless wickets caught behind or at slip.

Because you're so much slower through the air than other types of bowler, the problems of survival for the batsman are slightly different. Without having to make very fast decisions, he has more time to weigh up where and how hard he intends to hit the ball. This puts a premium on your accuracy. Without mastery of length and direction even the greatest spinner of the ball in the world would be annihilated.

Right at the outset you must decide which side of the wicket you're going to attack. You only have nine fielders at your disposition, and it's vital that you deploy them correctly. A good batting wicket means that you might have to outwait the batsman, maybe even buy a wicket or two. So try distributing your fielders in a six-three formation: six on the off side if you're a slow left-hander bowling just outside the off stump and six on the leg if you bowl off-breaks. If you're very accurate this can become seven-two, but in that case if you stray off line by the merest centimetre it'll be four runs almost for certain.

I firmly believe that all slow bowlers should have a slip fielder. Even in a defensive situation it's important to keep some pressure on the batsman. Without a slip, anything outside the off stump can be flashed at knowing with reasonable certainty that an edge will not go to hand. Depending on how much response there is from the wicket, or how heavily the odds are weighted in the batting side's favour, don't be afraid to crowd a batsman, particularly if he's new to the crease. In recent times the position of short silly point has become fashionable. It was originally devised by Brian Close, and suicidal though it may seem, particularly to those in the press box who are campaigning for legislation to prevent fielders from taking advantage of the extra protection given by crash-helmets to move closer to the batsman, it is, in fact, a relatively safe close-to-the-wicket fielding position because danger can be seen early and so evasive action is relatively simple.

The really lethal area is at short square leg, particularly if your side's off-spinner is not very accurate! Here there is no place to hide. Most bad fielding injuries in first-class cricket are sustained by the men who either show a foolhardy appetite for the position or who are 'volunteered' to stand there by their captains! It's a most important position for the off-spin bowler on a turning wicket, but if the ball is only turning a little, or very slowly, this short square leg fielder might well be better employed at silly mid-on, on the drive. However a good off-spinner always likes to bowl with a backward short leg, because he's looking to turn the ball enough to hit the inside edge of the bat.

Flight is the word used to describe the parabolic curve of the ball from the time it leaves the bowler's hand until it pitches. All the greatest spinners in history have possessed a teasing flight, and whatever some textbooks might tell you, it's easier for a short man to flight the ball than a tall man. On analysis this is obvious. A very tall person, say over six feet one inch, cannot afford to toss the ball even higher, for it will remain in the air too long and become easy meat for a quick-footed batsman. Also, a tall man often has greater difficulty in coordinating his limbs.

Consciously flighting the ball is not easy, but it is essential if you are to beat a batsman through the air, which can be just as destructive as turn off the pitch. A fast bowler regards flight as an

66

irrelevance. He's trying to get the ball from 'A' to 'B' in the shortest possible time. But for the slow bowler, it's a mighty useful arrow in the quiver, because the eyes of the batsman have to try to judge the curve of the ball's approach as well as its length and direction, so adding yet another problem to his survival. So if you're a slow bowler and practising hard in the nets, work on giving the ball an upward flick at release.

As a bowler, one of the first things you should look at in your opponent is the way he holds the bat. Generally speaking batsmen fall into one of the following grip categories. How they hold the bat inevitably affects the way they play.

(1) Those who grip the bat high up towards the end of the handle. These players are usually strong drivers, look to get on the front foot whenever possible, and do not have a great deal of control over the blade when playing defensively.

(2) Those who grip the bat low down near the splice. Generally this sort are good defenders with a preference for cutting and hooking. They often favour the back foot even when the ball's pitched well up.

(3) Those who grip the bat with their hands wide apart on the handle. This type of player very rarely hits the ball with any power, for his hands are working against one another. To force the ball away he needs exquisite timing, and when he does make a positive stroke the ball often goes in the air.

(4) Those who stand with the face of the bat turned well in towards their legs. Providing this is caused by the natural way in which the player grips the bat and is not an idiosyncrasy of his stance which is ironed out during his pick-up, such batsmen are invariably strong strikers of the ball on the leg side and good hookers and cutters. They find great difficulty however in hitting the well-pitched-up ball out in front of the wicket on the off side because the angle of the bat at impact forces the ball away to leg.

(5) Those who grip with an 'open' face to the bat – the opposite to the above. Excellent players on the off side and generally good in front of the wicket, but the angle of their bat

at impact means that any ball that moves across the face towards the slips may cause them to slice it to either the wicketkeeper or slips.

The way a batsman stands can often give away his intentions. Those with nearly all their weight on their back foot can only play forward with any degree of ease. Likewise, of course, those with a predominantly forward weight distribution prefer to play back wherever possible.

By reading the tips in this chapter, which because of the vast variety open to someone who wants to be an all-rounder is of necessity short and to the point, I hope you will find that analysis of opposing batsmen becomes a simpler operation. Certainly your awareness of what is in the batsman's mind plus knowledge of his strengths and weaknesses must help towards getting him out. Always try to put yourself into the boots of the man with the bat. In a very short time you will find this careful assessment of your opponent paying dividends.

3 Fielding – the Neglected Art

'Catches win matches' is an old cricketing cliché, but it is no less valid for all that. From village-green standard right up to the highest level, matches have been won by a single opportune catch. The recent success of the England team is in no small measure due to the fact that all of a sudden the close fielders started to catch most things above grass height. Ever since that moment, which began under Tony Greig's leadership in India, England's results have improved enormously. This was certainly the main difference between the England and Australian sides in the 1977 Test series in the UK.

But for some unfathomable reason fielding remains, comparatively speaking, the poor relation, left far behind in the accolades heaped on someone who takes six wickets or scores a hundred. Yet the man who might have done both these things can cost his side the game or at worst the series simply by dropping a vital catch towards the end of a match.

My own team, Glamorgan, won two county championships largely through the quality of their fielding. In 1948 a superb trio of short legs, Allan Watkins, Phil Clift and Wilfred Wooller, caught every half-chance offered from the inswing bowling of Norman Hever plus the off-breaks of Len Muncer and Johnny Clay. Only an average batting and bowling side, that particular team finished on top because these three catchers were well-nigh infallible, and were supported by sound, enthusiastic ground fielding. The 1969 championship XI which is the only side since the war to have gone through a season undefeated – and that includes the heavyweight Surrey and Yorkshire teams of the 1950s – was similar in the quality of its close catchers. We had four top-class performers close to the bat, and again our attack relied heavily on the inswing of Malcolm Nash and the off-spin of Don Shepherd. Between Roger Davis, Majid Khan, Brian Davis and myself we held 113 catches that season, and although our batting line-up was far stronger than the 1948 team, as we had Tony Lewis and Alan Jones as well as Majid Khan, it was the holding of half-chances and last-over snicks that won us the championship in the same year that Prince Charles was invested as Prince of Wales!

How Glamorgan won the 1969 County Championship – total concentration by all four close catchers: (left to right) the author, Majid (back to camera), Roger Davis making the catch, and Brian Davis covering behind his namesake

At no level of the game can any excuse be offered for the bad fielder. It is the one aspect at which even the biggest rabbit can become reasonably proficient through diligent practice. During the pre-season April nets, all first-class counties spend at least an hour a day working on the team's fielding, and each has its specialist performers in the vital close catching positions. But even without this high level of intensive practice there is no reason why even a club player should be a liability in the field, because it's the one facet of the game which you can practise alone. Bradman used to throw a golf ball against an uneven concrete wall and then hit the return with a stump. He also used this method to improve his fielding by sticking up a single wicket, throwing the ball against the wall and then trying to pick the return up cleanly and hit the stump with his throw.

More time is spent in the field than in any other part of the game. This being the case, it seems to me little short of incredible that general standards are so low. It can only mean two things. Firstly that not enough practice, and practice of a constructive rather than a haphazard kind, is being done. Secondly that the average level of fitness and athleticism isn't what it ought to be.

The fitter you are, the greater will be your suppleness and coordination – two major factors in dynamic fielding. Have you ever tried to have a short, sharp, close-catching fielding session while suffering from a hangover? If so, and take it from me I have bitter personal experience of this, the slowing-down in coordination between hand and eye is marked. A key factor in all fielding is alertness. In the course of a three-hour session in the field this will probably mean at least one catch being caught that wouldn't otherwise go to hand, and certainly a reduction of the number of runs scored by the opposition.

Of the ten ways in which a batsman can be dismissed, 'caught' must appear in more than half the entries in the scorebook. Breaking it down still further, catches close to the wicket must make up fifty to sixty per cent of this type of dismissal, so let's look first at this aspect, and if the bulk of this chapter deals with fielding close to the bat, I make no excuses.

CLOSE CATCHING

My own interest in this part of the game started way back in my schoolboy youth in South Africa. The MCC touring party of 1948/9 included the finest close catcher I have ever seen, Allan Watkins. As a twelve-year-old at Ellis Park, Johannesburg, I saw Allan, fielding at short square leg to the often erratic leg-spinner Doug Wright, dive far to his right and at full length catch a powerful pull from the South African captain, Dudley Nourse. The event burned an indelible print on my memory. Six years later, during a spell in the Merchant Navy, my ship called in to Cardiff. I decided to see if Glamorgan were playing and found my way to the county offices in the High Street. Opening the door, the first thing I saw was a framed picture of that catch. I knew then where my future lay.

In an odd way my two years at sea provided an invaluable if unusual grounding for my eventual eighteen-year association with Glamorgan. Crossing the Pacific from the Persian Gulf to Los Angeles, a journey taking three months at ten knots per hour, time went by very, very slowly. The ship in question was a Finnish tanker, and one of the other deckhands, a Dutchman, had played a bit of semi-professional baseball during a spell ashore in America. We met regularly on the open boat deck, upon which stood an enormous potato locker. We each took a side – usually me the port, he the starboard – and across the fifty-foot gap we would throw catches to each other using the locker as a source of missile supply. Inevitably potatoes would be hurled out of reach and disappear into the ocean. It was not long before we injected an element of competition into what had originally been just an idea to lighten the boredom. The throws gradually got flatter and quicker, wider and higher. We played 'sets'. First to get ten past the other won the set, only potatoes within genuine catching range to count.

The needle in these affairs makes me smile now, but the seriousness of the contest out there in the middle of nowhere, hundreds of miles from land and many thousands of miles away from any game of cricket, helped mould me into a close catcher who ended his career sixth in the list of all-time aggregate catchers in first-class cricket and third behind Wally Hammond and Mickey Stewart for the greatest number of catches ever held in one season!

As a suggestion, pinch a few potatoes from the larder and get someone to throw them at you. The variety of sizes and shapes make it very important not only that you catch them in exactly the right part of your hand – the base of your fingers – but that the way you recoil to take the speed off the potato must be spot-on too.

Out there on M/V *Aruba* our outfield was an iron deck, not grass, but such was the 'international' atmosphere the Dutchman and I created that we unhesitatingly dived full-length in our efforts to prevent the potatoes getting past! This helped me considerably in that other important close catching factor, the knack of being able to land well, rather like a gymnast, without either damaging oneself or jarring the ball out of one's hand.

(As a sort of PS. . . we ran out of potatoes two weeks out of Los Angeles, but by then the 'seed' had been sown!)

I was also fortunate to start my first-class career literally in between two of the best short leg fielders the game has ever known, my schoolboy hero Allan Watkins and Wilfred Wooller. Right through life we learn by imitating. Verbal advice is useful, but nowhere near so memorable as that which you actually see for yourself. So, if you're lucky enough to play in a side which has an exceptional fielder in its ranks, watch him closely, talk to him and try to find out how he's reached his high standards.

There are two basic requisites for becoming a first-rate close-to-the-wicket catcher. They are a set of fast reflexes which can be speeded up still further by practice and conditioning by regular spells of fielding in the one position, and a pair of 'balanced' eyes. Let me hastily reassure you that clarity of vision and balanced eyes are two altogether separate things. There have been many fine batsmen who wore glasses; in his prime Mike Smith, the former England captain and Warwickshire batsman, was also a magnificent short leg fielder.

Not long after I'd found that I had a natural aptitude for

Solkar has anticipated Brearley's forward defensive push against the slow left-hand bowling of Bedi and moved forward to take the catch as the ball is played

fielding close to the bat and had begun to build something of a reputation in the game for some of the chances I was hanging on to, I was sent to a leading optician as part of a nationwide survey into what made different sportsmen supreme in their particular field. What I'm about to relate is the specialist's report and his interpretation, in optical terms, of why I could catch as well as I could.

It seems that human beings initially see an object as two separate images, one for each eye. It only takes a moment to align the two into one, and so fast does this take place that very very few are aware of the time-lag involved. But in that split second which it takes the ball to travel from the bat to the fielder, his eyes have to reconcile the two images into one and at the same time relay to his

74

brain and on to his limbs information concerning the speed of the oncoming object. This 'binocular vision' as it's known in optometry is necessary before the fielder can accurately direct his hands into a catching position on the same plane as the ball. If yours are perfectly synchronized, or 'balanced', this correction and estimation happens much quicker than in people with a slight defect in vision or perhaps one eye marginally stronger than the other. In such cases the ball will either speed past the fielder before he moves – this can also happen to someone with balanced eyes if it passes him faster than his reaction time – or else his brain will order his hands to move into slightly the wrong position. (How often have you seen a ball pass either just over or under a fielder's outstretched hand?)

The end of a great innings. Gary Cosier at short square leg only reached this bat/pad edge because his weight was well forward on the balls of his feet

75

Richie Robinson, normally a wicketkeeper, showing the elementary lesson that two hands are twice as safe as one!

I am fortunate enough to have a pair of 'balanced eyes'. So too I'm sure have Bobby Simpson the Australian, Phil Sharpe, Tony Lock and Graham Roope. For us the ball virtually leaves the bat as a single object, thus greatly reducing that split second of eye indecision. This factor not only gives us that little bit of extra time – and we're talking here in milli-seconds – but immediately directs our hands to the same planc as the onrushing ball.

Size of hands is not as important as one might think. The Bedser twins had the proverbial buckets for hands, but neither was particularly noted for his safeness in the field. Allan Watkins on the other hand – if you'll pardon the pun – had small, pudgy palms with short stubby fingers.

Just as in batting and bowling, rhythm and timing play a big part in making a successful catch. This I'm afraid is inborn. Ball sense cannot be acquired by practice alone. Watch a good fielder, even one who operates away from the bat, and you'll notice that the ball somehow seems to melt into his hands, irrespective of the pace at which it approaches him. This is timing, the instinctive ability to adjust the amount of recoil the hands need to slow up and finally absorb the ball. To the finest catchers, how hard the ball has been struck at them poses no insurmountable problem, for they all have this inborn rhythm.

Anticipation plays a major part in becoming an efficient *out-fielder* where twos can be turned into singles time and time again with a shrewd reading of the batsman's stroke. Much has been written of 'wonderfully anticipated catches close to the wicket . . .' But in this area, forethought is a dangerous and unreliable companion to anyone who wants to become a consistent performer in this area. Take this as an example of what I mean.

As the bowler starts his run up the fielder crouches, knees flexed, hands held loosely in front of him about two feet off the ground, palms facing towards the batsman. With the weight on the balls of his feet he's on balance ready to set off in any direction high or low, left or right. As the ball is about to be played, and in this case edged, the fielder should be motionless, still crouched, head still, waiting for his eyes to instruct his hands and body and

78

completely free to let his reflexes do the work. Why crouched? Because it's easier to stand up suddenly than to bend down from an upright position. Such a close catcher has a marvellous chance of catching that edge.

Now suppose anticipation gets into the act! Our fielder, having seen the intended stroke before impact, believes the ball is going to be deflected away to his left and so starts to move in this direction. But no human being can judge just how thin an edge the batsman will get. Take the backward short leg position as our example. A wafer-thin brush of the inside edge of the bat will send the ball to the right of our fielder, who, remember, is all set to go to his left.

Wood edges Lillee through the slips as all are rooted to the spot

Even if he hasn't actually moved an inch but merely assumed in his mind that the ball will be deflected to his left, he has no chance whatsoever of catching that particular ball. You see his muscles are now programmed to go left, and a reversal of instruction as his eyes tell him otherwise will leave him momentarily paralysed. The ball is only in catching range for a half a second at most, so another chance has gone begging.

Anticipation results in more catches being missed close to the wicket than it gobbles up. You have only a half-chance of being right, so why not, as in batting and bowling, leave it to your eyes to decide?

Knott edges the ball through the slips/gulley – all the close fielders have rocked back on their heels, anticipating the fierce slash of Knott's stroke. They are in no position to catch anything other than a ball at chest height or above

To be a first-class close fielder you should be able to catch the ball cleanly and surely with either hand. All of us favour one side, so in practice make a point at working on your weaker flank. Of course there's no substitute for endless repetition practising. It's rather like that necessary chore that faces musicians, scale practice. If you can't find someone to join you either on a wooden cradle, by hitting you catches, or by sharing in some close-range hand-to-hand stuff, then a few pounds spent on one of those nylon mesh catching nets is certainly a good investment.

A little trick I used to use before going out will probably be of some use in sharpening your reflexes. The quicker your reactions the easier you will make that vital catch. Take two tenpenny pieces and lay them on the flat of your hand with your arm extended in front of you at shoulder height. One coin should be near the tips of your fingers, the other towards the base of your palm. With a slight upward flick of your rigid arm, not just the hand, push the coins into the air. Then quickly turn your hand over, palm now facing towards the ground, and grab them *one at a time* as they drop downwards. You should be able to reclaim both before they reach waist height.

Two coins shouldn't pose much of a problem. Now try three, with the extra coin near the roots of the fingers. When you can catch four with either hand (the extra one should be placed on your wrist) with the rules described, then you will have sharpened your speed and coordination of hand and eye to rival the greatest close fielders the game has known.

Most close catchers prefer to field on one side of the wicket. Try the slips and then the short leg positions for yourself. You can experiment during a practice match. Once you've found the place where you feel happiest, try to become something of a specialist there.

A lot has been written about whether to watch the bat or the ball from the bowler's hand. Try both and see which you prefer. There are no hard-and-fast rules, but my experience is that it's better to watch the edge of the bat from the off-side position and a spot around the batsman's front knee from short leg. I recom-

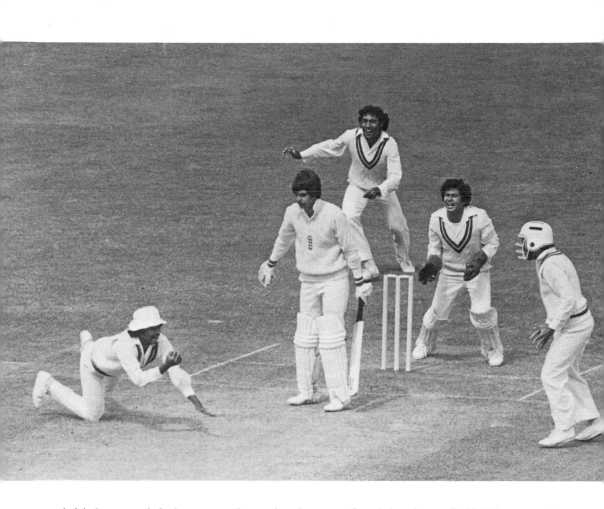

mend this because it helps to cut down the chances of anticipating wrongly by following the ball's progress down the wicket before the batsman has actually made contact.

Attempt to catch everything, no matter how far away or improbable it may appear. Otherwise there will be too many times when a ball will pass you by and on reflection you'll realize it was within reach if you'd tried first time.

You should spend as long on improving your fielding as you do batting and bowling.

Geoff Miller unnerved by the closeness of the fielders; Sadiq at short square leg wearing the newly fashionable protective helmet

83

OUTFIELDING

Your greatest contribution is to keep the opposition's score down to the barest mimimum. Once again specialization will bring improved performance. I know it's not difficult to doze off partially if the ball isn't hit in your direction very often, but like the close catcher you should be prepared for every ball to be hit your way. The time for relaxing and looking at the passing boundary parade is when the bowler is walking back to his mark ... although a captain attempting to make a slight undetected alteration to his field won't thank me for saying that!

Anticipation away from the wicket is a *must*. This is especially the case in the areas twenty to thirty yards from the bat, i.e. cover and mid-wicket. Limited-over cricket has turned these two positions into the most important ones on the field. Men like Gower and Radley can often save twenty runs in a forty-over match. Here you need agility and speed across the ground. You don't require the strongest throwing arm in the world, but accuracy of return to the stumps and a cool head when there's a chance of a run out are vital.

I've always been surprised why more fielders in these run-saving yet attacking positions haven't developed the ability to throw in with both arms. It seems elementary to me that unless you've the physique and skill to throw off-balance like a Clive Lloyd, then two-handedness is as important a factor in the outfield as being able to catch securely with either hand is to a close-to-the-wicket fielder. The other attribute you need within the positions thirty yards from the bat is to be able to pick up and throw at the wicket underarm, preferably in one smoth movement with the minimum of wind-up – Viv Richards, the West Indian, changed the course of the 1975 World Cup Final with run-outs of this type. In the event of a quickly taken single, a swift underhand flick, even if it's along the ground, will get the ball back to the wickets far more quickly than a full overarm pelt.

Always throw towards the end to which the slowest batsman is running. This may sound elementary but it's surprising how many shies are directed to the wrong end. It's all part of being alert and concentrating on the job. Never stand still while the ball is being played. It's useless to walk in and then stop as the ball is struck. By being in motion you're in a better position to accelerate inwards or turn and chase. Watch Graham Barlow of Middlesex and Derek Randall of Nottingham, two marvellous examples of this part of the art of fielding.

When walking in as the bowler runs up, keep your eyes on the batsman. He will telegraph where he wants to hit the ball, and if you read him correctly you may just be able to cut off the stroke. If it's been played off the back foot and they call for a quick single, the man who struck the ball will almost always take longer to get to safety at the bowler's end than the other batsman. If in doubt, throw to the end nearest you, but never blindly. By keeping on your toes and weighing up the situation ball by ball you'll make the right decision more times than not.

The best way to pick up the ball on the run so that you can return it as fast as possible is to make sure (if you're right-handed) that your *right* foot is forward carrying the weight of your body as you stoop to pick up the ball. You then only have to throw your left foot and weight forward as you stand up and the ball is on its way. If you pick it up with your left foot forward you'll have to take another step with your right before you can wind up for the throw.

Here again cricket is a sideways game. Point the left hand at the target, and when you throw, try to let the ball go rather like a javelin thrower. This way there's far less strain on the shoulder ligaments and muscle fibres. If you throw from shoulder height and somewhat roundarm, one day you'll damage those fibres and your days as a long-distance thrower are over. Through throwing incorrectly, many, many first-class cricketers suffer from this affliction.

Many catches in the outfield are straightforward, but every ground has a slight difference in its background. So before a match, go and have a few practice catches facing in different directions to get the 'feel'. Also have a look where the sun is and bear in mind the direction in which it will sink. Always try to get

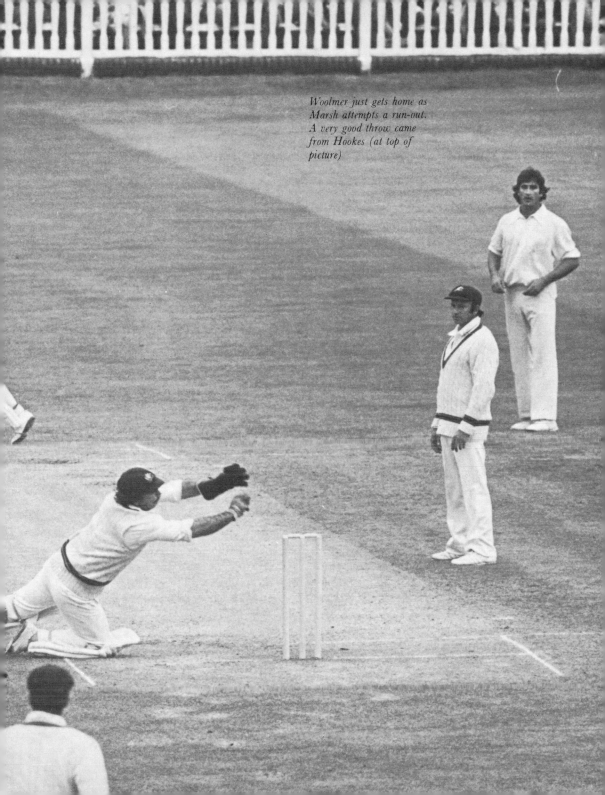

Woolmer just gets home as Marsh attempts a run-out. A very good throw came from Hookes (at top of picture)

behind the ball if you can. If you fumble it then you may have a chance of catching the rebound as it bounces off your body. If a skier comes your way, don't charge in until your eyes have weighed up the height and approximate landing area of the ball. Many chances are missed because a fielder sees the ball get hit in his direction and goes charging in, only to find he's completely misjudged it and it's gone over his head. Remember, it is always easier to run in fast than travel backwards.

The ideal position for your hands as the ball enters is close together with the fingers pointing at roughly 45° horizontally

Ross Edwards throws in. His left arm originally pointed at the wickets. The throw is made against the braced left leg, which helps both distance and accuracy

away from the path of the oncoming ball. Little fingers crossed (thumbs if the ball is being caught above head height). For a high dropping catch keep your hands up so that when the ball arrives they're around shoulder height. As the ball enters, bring your hands in towards your body, making sure that your elbows pass either side of your midriff.

Unless a side holds on to its chances it can never hope to achieve anything other than erratic success. If you want to be an all-rounder worthy of the name then your fielding standards should be as high as in the other two skills. There are three strings to an all-rounder's bow, so remember, even if you haven't had a world-shattering day as a batsman or bowler, you can still make a telling contribution in the field.

Iqbal catches Amarnath, Second Test, Pakistan v. India 1978. Note Iqbal's total concentration and the high position of his hands. The ball was eventually caught around shoulder height

4 Make the Most of Yourself

This book is aimed specifically at the all-rounder and mainly at those who have already got a reasonable grasp of the basics. Many of you will have read thousands of words about the technical aspects of batting and bowling and spent hours in the nets taking advice and trying to graft it on to your own game. In other fields even sportsmen of the calibre of Borg, Nicklaus, Beckenbauer and Muhammad Ali go through periods when they need to re-examine their technique and turn to outside help. This is not weakness on their parts. It is a simple fact of sporting life – particularly in ball games – that small errors do unconsciously creep in, and with error comes uncertainty, followed closely by a loss of confidence leading more often than not to defeat.

So the basics in this book have been pretty basic. What I've attempted to do is to give one or two fundamental checkpoint areas and then concentrate on ways of exploring and developing your talents.

Unlike fast bowlers, all-rounders come in all shapes and sizes. In the main they are medium-pacers or orthodox spinners, with the odd rarity like Mushtaq Mohammed, who is a leg-spinner, Imran Khan, who can be genuinely quick, and the daddy of them all, Sir Garfield Sobers, who was literally everything in one!

So this book is not intended as an all-rounder's encyclopedia, there to be hauled out of a dusty shelf whenever a problem needs solving. Like betting on horses, driving home a point in print so that it bears fruit is often a matter of luck. Somewhere among the many thousands of words that you have read on the game there may be the odd phrase or suggestion that has proved helpful to you personally. If so, you're fortunate. But in the end, you're on your own. Batting against a Bob Willis or Dennis Lillee or Wayne Daniel is a lonely occupation. No elaborate theory in the world is going to be of any use to you once the missile's on its way. You need to have a solid technique and a sound mental approach to survive and succeed. Similarly, if Mike Procter or some such is in full cry with the bat, no bowler on earth is going to keep him quiet.

But being an all-rounder has enormous compensations, for you need never be completely out of the game. Surprisingly, a bad run with the bat and loss of length and line with the ball rarely come together. No one has successfully explained why this should be, unless it's a case of the player in question subconsciously applying himself that little bit harder in one department than the other. My own experience is that if one has some success with, say, the bat then it's psychologically that much harder to motivate oneself with the ball. The finest all-rounders, the Soberses, the Procters, the Bothams, seem to be able to separate this twin existence so that mentally they compete as keenly as if they had had a miserable failure with their other skill.

At a lower level, the best way to succeed is to quickly realize your own limitations and then play within them. If you're a good cutter of the ball but weak on the leg side then wait until an opportunity presents itself to use your strength. Be content to push and nudge singles elsewhere. You may want to be a fast bowler and have the right killer instinct and action. But if you haven't been blessed with the inborn ability to bowl quick then throttle back to a more sedate pace where success probably awaits you. If you cannot throw a cricket ball accurately and with a flat trajectory more than thirty yards and are rather short on speed around the park, try to become a specialist fielder nearer the bat.

Above all you must always retain a true perspective of your talents in order to develop them to their utmost.

Peter Richardson, the former Worcestershire, Kent and England opening batsman who scored 44 hundreds and 25,000 first-class runs, including 2000 in Test matches, once remarked that he

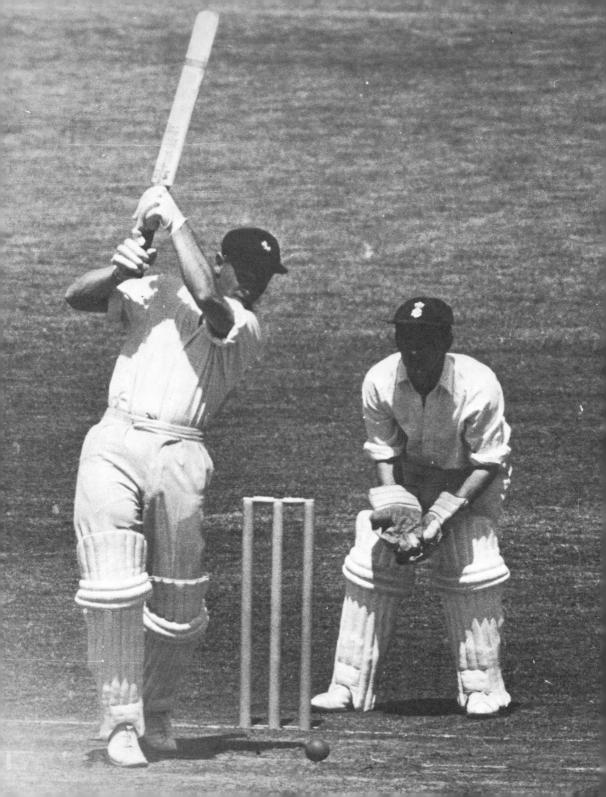

only had four scoring strokes! He waited until the right ball came along and then bingo! In spite of these self-imposed restrictions Peter rarely became bogged down, because he was a pastmaster at deflecting and working the ball away for singles if the bowlers did not bowl within his scoring arc.

Always make sure that your equipment is the best you can afford. I know prices have gone through the roof, but without a good bat, for instance, you just cannot hope to succeed. A good bat is not automatically the highest-priced. Picking one can be a hit-and-miss affair. Even knowledgeable first-class batsmen make mistakes picking out a bat. You can be sure of only two things before you actually use it. Make sure that the handle is a comfortable thickness – Clive Lloyd has five grips on his to bring it up to what *he* feels is right – and be happy with the way the bat picks up. This last point is impossible to put into words. Modern bats can weigh anything from 2lb 3oz up to around the 3lb mark. Some at the heavier end of the scale will 'feel' much lighter than a bat 10 oz less on the scales. This is largely to do with the centre of gravity of the bat and its balance. Herein lies the bat maker's art. There are a lot of gimmicks around at the moment – scooped-out backs, thickened edges, even holes drilled through the blade. They *may* work, but don't be misled into thinking that a newfangled idea is the answer to a batting average of 10! Also remember, although you can be lucky or unlucky with the driving qualities of the bat you've just purchased, whatever you do, don't for heaven's sake buy one that is too heavy. Try an assortment of bats in your sports shop before making up your mind, and if you're lucky enough to know a first-class player personally, ask him. His advice will invariably be sound.

Don't over-oil your new bat. Oil is a preservative only, it does nothing at all to improve a bat's driving capabilities. Just a smear over the face, edges and back two or three times will be enough. Keep it away from the splice as this will loosen the glue. Sandpaper the face and edges clean after every session in the nets or middle. This helps to prevent nicks on the edge from splitting still further. Surface cracks on the face of the bat are a sign of high-quality willow, so don't be upset if these appear – they have no effect on the bat's performance. Try to ensure that the bat's first half-hour of initial use is against an old ball, but with today's manufacturing techniques, even this is not essential. If you don't want to over-concern yourself with looking after the blade, then by all means consider buying one with a polyurethane or plastic finish. These only need a wipe with a damp cloth to keep them looking in trim, and of course you don't have to bother about oiling!

Buy the lightest pads you can. They are for protection only, and you don't want to be saddled with the kind of weight Red Rum had on his back in the National. Boots too should be light and comfortable. There's a fad around at the moment for boots shaped like plimsolls. This is all right for specialist batsmen, although they don't give much protection against a fast inswinging yorker, but an all-rounder needs something more substantial, a slightly thicker sole and a boot that goes some way up the ankle for support while bowling. Take care of your gear. It will repay a little attention, like making sure it's dry before being packed away, by lasting a lot longer.

Wear decent thick socks, preferably woollen. A lot of professional players wear two pairs. If you're on your feet for most of the day on spiked boots, you'll be glad of the extra padding, particularly if the grounds are hard.

Unless you play on some terribly unreliable wickets – if so I suggest you either move to a different club or take up golf – then you almost certainly won't need a crash helmet! But make sure you buy a box with a padded edge, and if you feel a thigh pad is an unnecessary expense, a folded towel draped over your jockstrap will do the job just as well and will probably be more comfortable too.

Above all, practise methodically. This applies to all parts of the game. There is no point in getting into the nets for a ten-minute caper. Your batting habits are formed here. Make sure they are good ones. If you have a particular problem that is causing your dismissal most weekends, ask the bowlers to concentrate on that type of delivery. Play each practice session as if it were an actual match.

Clubs should make it a rule one night a week that the first time a batsman is dismissed in practice he makes way for the next. Try too to hold the odd session out in the middle as if it were for real. Get into the routine of offering a pint of beer on your wicket – and paying for it at the end of nets if someone has bowled you out! The most uncertain part of any innings is the first twenty minutes, so try to utilize your net practice to improve your technique so that you can survive this period.

A good temperament is a must if you are to succeed consistently. Everyone is nervous before an occasion so loaded with uncertainty as batting. Even hardened internationally known entertainers like Harry Secombe and David Frost admit to getting butterflies before going out to bat in a Sunday charity match. Temperament is either something inherent which makes you lift your own game to meet the challenge or hopefully something you develop with growing experience. It might well be summed up as the ability to analyse a situation and respond to it in a positive controlled way.

The only help I can offer here is to suggest that while batting you play each and every ball as a completely separate problem from the one that preceded it, irrespective of whether it just shaved the off stump or, more dangerous still, has just been retrieved from a nearby brewer's yard where you dispatched it! Block out the picture of the crouching fielders, particularly those in front of the bat who may well be there purely as a decoy for your concentration rather than as a reflection of the state of the wicket.

Get a working knowledge of the laws of the game. They run to sixteen small-print pages at the back of Wisden's Almanack each year, but a grasp of them will increase your understanding of the game and will help to make you a better 'all-round' player. The same applies to a knowledge of the game's history. Your library will have any amount of literature on this. The most comprehensive treatise available is E. W. Swanton's and Michael Melford's massive *The World of Cricket*, but a more concise and useful recent history is *English Cricket — the Game and Its Players Through the Ages* by Christopher Brookes. It's no bad thing to be aware of the heritage that you are helping to perpetuate.

Most important, believe in yourself. Modesty is part of the game's great charm, and long may it remain. But inwardly you must have a strength of purpose in excess of the eleven men who are trying to defeat you. All the great teams in history have had an unmistakable air of authority about them. So too have the best sides in your Saturday afternoon competitions.

The way to combine all your attributes into one is to master the basic techniques, equip yourself with some tactical knowledge of the game, and go into each match with an inner conviction that you and your team are better than the opposition or at the very least in with a sporting chance.

The best way to reap the maximum amount of enjoyment from your exertions is to be proficient in the skills required. Cricket is a great leveller. I know that this claim is made by a number of sports, but possibly nowhere else can a greater sense of frustration, or of elation, be manifested than along a twenty-two yard strip of turf.

As an all-rounder your opportunities for both are double. Make the most of them and savour the latter!

5 The Great All-Rounders of Our Time

Looking around the world at the current crop of all-rounders, several names demand inclusion in this chapter. When one can look back at the eras that spawned Keith Miller, Vinoo Mankad, Richie Benaud, Alan Davidson, Trevor Bailey, Ray Illingworth and Trevor Goddard, the cupboard does not perhaps now seem as full, but before a quick look at the skills and attitudes of some of the leading present-day all-rounders, no book on the subject could go into print without an analysis of the 'Supreme Being', Sir Garfield Sobers.

GARY SOBERS

Sobers was a freak, a cricketing genius, a top-class performer in every department with no real weakness. The quality that made him so remarkable was his ability to bowl virtually every form of delivery from the genuinely quick bouncer to chinamen and googlies. Even here he was different, for he had at least two ways of bowling the 'wrong 'un' – the one he wanted you to 'read' from his hand and the other which was practically indistinguishable from his chinaman off-spinner. To add to all this he was of course left-handed, a plus factor which gave the great man a ten-per-cent advantage over everyone else before he'd bowled a ball or taken strike.

As a batsman Sobers combined a superb technique with great power and a delicate touch. His every movement, even while walking back to his bowling mark, was fluid and graceful – at times he scarcely seemed to have a bone in his body – but the whiplash steel was there when needed.

He came to the United Kingdom in 1957 as a raw, nineteen-year-old, slow left-hand bowler who'd come to learn. Within two years he was the best all-round cricketer the world has ever seen. His Test match figures dwarf all others.

Bowling against Gary was both a pleasure and painful. Like so many West Indians he appeared somewhat 'loose', especially when stretching forward defensively. But in this very looseness lay his strength, for he was able to make rapid last-second adjustments to meet a sudden problem created by the ball so that he never appeared to be either out of position or in a hurry – a sure sign of class. He had every stroke in the book, from the lofted drive over cover to the hook, and had the great batsmen's ability to strike two seemingly identical balls to different parts of the field. When in full cry this made it well-nigh impossible to place a field to him. He also, and this is rare in an all-rounder, had the concentration to play a long innings and was ultra-reliable in a crisis.

As a bowler, few in modern times have been able to swing the new ball so prodigiously. When the mood took him he could be almost as quick as Wesley Hall! Test bowling is all about accuracy, and a world-class rhythm is as delicately balanced as the movement of a fine Swiss watch. Not so Sobers. Almost without pause he could turn from his faster method into an orthodox slow left-hander. There immediately would be the artful flight and considerable finger-spin. A few overs later he could switch to that hardest variety to control, unorthodox wrist spin with a variety of top-spin and googlies added to the pile.

As a fielder he was one of the game's supreme short legs, and in concert with off-spinner Lance Gibbs he set new standards here too. He was criticized as a captain, but nearly always on the grounds that he would take unjustifiable risks in an effort to win. To cap it all, the man had inner humility about his incredible prowess and a level of sportsmanship that can only be described

OPPOSITE *Sobers bowling — what balance, what venom!*

LEFT *Making it look so easy: Luckhurst ct. Sobers b. Julien, Third Test, England* v. *West Indies, 1973*

as 'amateurish' in the purest sense of the word.

No one looks ever likely to approach Bob Beamon's twenty-nine-foot long jump at the Mexico Olympics. It's a record that will last out the century at least. So too does Sobers stand supreme, a King amongst Princes.

Test matches	Runs	HS	100s	Av.	Wickets	Av.	Catches
93	8032	365*	26	57.78	235	34.03	109

101

IAN BOTHAM

Twenty-three-year-old Ian Botham is now being compared with the youthful Sobers. The lad from Somerset has had a remarkable Test career which in a short space of time has already established him (inside or outside Packer cricket) as arguably the best all-rounder in the world.

In his early days as a professional Ian was often too headstrong, particularly with the bat. No one doubted his power or inherent skills, but there were strong reservations about his ability to harness them. Now he is a big-occasion cricketer, raising his game to meet the importance of the match. The 1978 Gillette Cup final was a good example of this, when his innings of 80 was the highest of the day even though he finished on the losing side.

As a batsman, Ian is far sounder against medium-pace and fast bowling than spin. Technically he has several defensive flaws, particularly when playing forward against a quality spinner, but his enormous strength frequently gets him out of trouble should he mishit a drive. He gets most of his runs off the front foot, and inside the game is reckoned to be the hardest English-born striker of the ball since Ted Dexter retired.

Ian has been fortunate to play in an England side which has rarely needed to get very big scores either to win or to stay in the game. Brought up in the county one-day atmosphere, his approach with the bat is very much that of 'up and at 'em!' His hundreds in Test cricket have always been offensive rather than match-saving ones, and in the latter situation his defensive limitations make him somewhat vulnerable. But with his eye in, Botham can destroy an attack very much in the manner of his Somerset team mate, the West Indian Viv Richards.

As a bowler Ian is unrecognizable from the lad who aped the gentle medium pace of his one-time county mentor, Tommy Cartwright. Almost overnight the big fella added three yards of pace to go with his developing skill at swinging the ball. He puts it down to the 1976 winter which he spent playing and coaching in Australian club cricket. Bowling on true pitches improved his

OPPOSITE *The muscular power of Ian Botham. His strength enables him to pulverize just-short-of-a-length bowling*

102

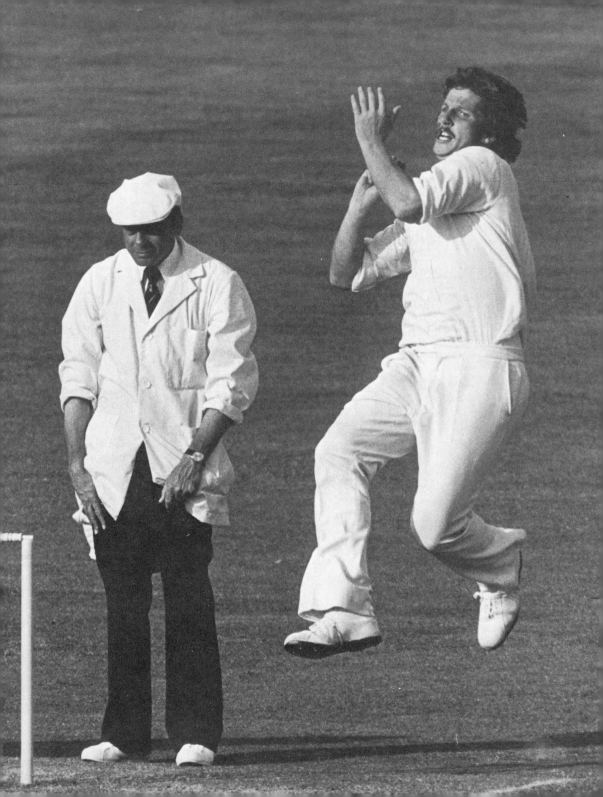

command of length and line, and the need to bang the ball harder into the pitch than the green fields of home to get any response brought out the untapped reserves of pace that had lain dormant until then.

The departure of Cartwright and Brian Close and the dwindling powers of medium-pacer Graham Burgess thrust more responsibility upon him, and because he is by nature a blood-and-guts performer, the result was an overnight England-class all-rounder. In county cricket he has a tendency to over-use the bouncer, and has been known to lose his cool so that he gets wild and erratic. But in Test matches he is an absolute model. 87 wickets in 17 Tests have come about through the most devastating exhibition of swing bowling since Bob Massie took 16 England wickets in the Lords match in 1972.

ABOVE *Haworth ct. Botham b. Hendrick. (Second Test, England v. New Zealand, 1978). Note how Botham's knees have provided the springy 'cushion' needed to take the pace off a fast-flying edge*

OPPOSITE *Botham showing the aggressive instinct which has made him one of the world's leading all-rounders*

105

Ian's harvest of wickets happened because he concentrates on pitching the ball right up to the bat. The longer the ball is in the air, the more and later in its flight it is likely to swing. By committing the batsman to the front foot his awayswinger searches for the outside edge, while the lateness of his inswinger and the disguising of the change of delivery has trapped many an experienced Test batsman lbw. In Test matches Ian uses the bouncer with more discretion because he's an intelligent enough cricketer to realize that at his pace the truer batting strips for five-day matches give a well-set batsman plenty of time to fasten onto a short-pitched delivery.

Botham has great heart, and a confidence in himself and his ability which is understandably pretty substantial after his rapid rise to the top. This is not to say that he is a braggart or lacks charm – far from it – but all the best sportsmen have a certain arrogance, and his record to date is such that in his case it's most certainly not misplaced.

A safe catcher, particularly at slip, he's not only taken Tony Greig's position in the England team but is now also to be found lurking where Greig did in the silly mid-off position to Edmonds, Miller and Emburey. Ian also has one attribute without which no cricketer rises above the average. He is extraordinarily lucky. Add that ingredient to his make-up and it's easy to see why he's the most exciting and entertaining all-round talent in world cricket at the moment.

Test matches	Runs	HS	100s	Av.	Wickets	Av.	Catches
17	791	108	3	35·95	87	18·68	21

MUSHTAQ MOHAMMED

OPPOSITE Mushtaq Mohammad – no doubting the little man's courage, right behind the ball. Note how deep Alan Knott is standing

Mushtaq comes from a remarkable family of five brothers, four of whom have played for Pakistan. Yet only Mushtaq of the five has any pretensions to being a bowler. He was the youngest Test cricketer ever – only fifteen years 124 days when he played against the West Indies at Lahore in the 1958/9 series. Two years earlier,

at the incredible age of just thirteen, he had made his first-class debut for Karachi Whites against Hyderabad, scoring 87 and taking 5 for 87 with his leg-breaks and googlies! Before he was nineteen he had scored two Test centuries, and he went on to captain Pakistan before opting for the Packer circus, a decision which made his Board of Control strip him of the leadership, only to reinstate him a year later, after public pressure, for the vital series against India.

Mushtaq's qualities are perhaps not quite so obvious as those of, say, Sobers or Botham. Like so many cricketers from the sub-continent, finesse rather than force is his forte. Only five feet five inches tall, but sturdily built, for a small man he hits the ball with surprising power, but because of his stature this comes mainly through timing rather than effort. Like all the Mohammeds he has an idiosyncratic little twirl of the bat as he takes guard, but the blade is pretty straight once the ball's on its way!

Mushtaq has fine powers of concentration. Long hours in the dazzling sunshine pose major problems in fixing the mind solely on the ball for any length of time. He does this superbly, and the patience which his race seems to have in abundance coupled with a fine defensive technique have been repaid with over fifty first-class hundreds, including five double centuries and one score over 300.

Mushtaq also has the gene without which no amount of talent would be successful: he has courage. Watch him play genuine fast bowling. Occasionally he might jump in the air, but then with his height it is not always easy to get over the bounce of the ball to keep it down. But he's right behind the line of the ball. Like so many of his countryman he's a beautiful, wristy cutter of anything slightly short or wide, and he has perfected a stroke which no other first-class cricketer attempts – a kind of reverse backhand smash through the slips. He uses this with totally demoralizing effect to a slow bowler pitching consistently wide of his off stump.

With a ball in his hand he is no less of a competitor. Many of the world's finest leg-spinners have been short men – 'Tich' Freeman and Clarrie Grimmett, for instance. To spin the ball a lot it helps

OPPOSITE *Certainly a googly on its way from Mushtaq here: you can tell this by the position of his right wrist. Like all fine bowlers he is beautifully balanced*

108

to let it go with a slightly upwards trajectory, and Mushtaq does this with great cunning. He also has the googly and the 'flipper' the fast, flat ball which skids on after pitching. Learning to bowl on the perfect batting strips of Pakistan has given Mushtaq a high level of control over this most difficult form of bowling. Without it a leg-spinner would be murdered. Only the quality of his batting stopped this genuine all-rounder from developing into one of the best leg-spinners of all time.

Nimble in the field, with a safe pair of hands, Mushtaq quickly realized that without the ability to throw the ball very far he would have to become a specialist close-to-the-wicket catcher. His characteristic tenacity, practice and commitment have made him highly competent in this department too.

Test matches	Runs	HS	100s	Av.	Wickets	Av.	Catches
55	3,555	201	10	39·94	79	28·25	41

The above figures are correct as at 1 March 1979, the time of going to press, i.e. they do not include Pakistan's two Tests v. Australia in March.

MIKE PROCTER

Procter is one of those rare birds, a fast-bowling all-rounder. He is such a versatile performer that at the height of his powers, before his serious knee injury in 1975, he was often called the 'white Sobers'. The comparison was by no means far-fetched.

As a boy, Procter was lucky in many ways. With his considerable natural talent for games, he could have been an international-class performer at rugby, hockey, tennis or squash. He was fortunate to have parents wealthy enough to send him to Hilton College, one of the best public schools in South Africa. There a strong sporting tradition helped to nurture and develop a talent that was bursting to come out. You may be surprised to know that at school, one of the post-war period's fastest bowlers was a wicketkeeper! At the age of eleven he scored five centuries one season, including an innings of 210!

So there has never been any question that Michael John Procter

OPPOSITE *Mike Procter showing the kind of controlled aggression that makes him such a formidable opponent*

110

had the right ingredients for greatness. He came to the United
Kingdom in 1963 as a member of a South African schoolboy team,
spent a year on the Gloucestershire staff on trial, and then joined
them full-time in 1968. In ten years he has received virtually every
honour in the game. One of Wisden's five Cricketers of the Year in
1970, co-holder of the world record for the most consecutive
first-class hundreds in a row – six – and since 1977, captain of
Gloucestershire. Because of South Africa's racial policies his Test
match appearances have been limited to just seven, all against
Australia in 1966 and 1969, but he appeared as of right in the Rest
of the World team who played England in 1970 as a replacement
series for the cancelled South African tour.

Procter's batting method is classically simple. Primarily a
front-foot player, during the early part of an innings he attempts
very little except to push forward defensively, bat and pad close
together. He rarely picks his bat up higher than his waist, and
someone who had never seen him in full flow could be deceived
into thinking that here was just another competent county hack.
But once the reconnoitring is done, the method remains just as
methodical, the pick-up gets higher, and the power becomes
awesome. The South African hits the ball in the air more safely
than anyone else in the modern game, not just aiming for a six, but
to place the ball studiously out of a fielder's reach. Because of this,
when set he is quite impossible to bowl at, and is a captain's
despair when it comes to field placing. He scores at an extraordinarily quick rate, yet there is nothing hurried or violent about the
way he sets about the bowler's assassination. A glance at the
Procter physique explains why brute force is unnecessary. He's
built like the proverbial brick outhouse, solid from the ground up.

This great natural strength contains the secret of how he can
bowl so fast with such an awkward action. He lets the ball go off
the wrong foot, is chest-on at delivery and is too wide of the crease
for the purists – in short he defies all recognized orthodox
methods. Some fast bowlers can bowl just as quick off a fifteen-
yard run-up as thirty. Not so Procter. He uses every inch of his
enormous run. Not for him a smooth, gliding approach. He

charges in like a Pamplona bull. He needs as much forward impetus as possible in order to deliver the ball fast, and when this running speed is coupled to the whirlwind action of his arm, whose force is generated from a pair of shoulders that would have done Sonny Liston proud, the combination releases a projectile that sets off in the region of 90 mph!

Since his knee trouble Procter has bowled fast only in rare bursts. But such is his all-round talent that he can now switch to deceptively gentle-looking off-spinners with some effect.

Like many cricketers from Britain's former colonies, he is a hard, tearaway opponent on the field – almost as if he has something to prove every ball. His captaincy lifted Gloucestershire to the heights of a Benson and Hedges Cup final in 1977, and like all the best captains, he leads from the front by personal example. A brilliant slip fielder, and the most modest and unassuming of men off the field, his absence from the Test arena because of political forces outside his control is one of the tragedies of the modern game.

Test matches	Runs	HS	100s	Av.	Wickets	Av.	Catches
7	226	48	0	25.11	41	15.02	4

TONY GREIG

Whatever his failings in the eyes of establishment cricket, Tony Greig deserves to be included in this short résumé of world-class all-rounders. It is true that his performances have rapidly fallen away since his association with Kerry Packer, but the outside pressures put on this engaging if occasionally infuriating six-foot-seven-inch all-rounder were greater than upon any other cricketer in history.

Tony is here in this book because he is the most combative all-rounder of them all. He answers fire with fire, and his performances in Australia in 1974/5, when Thomson and Lillee went through the bulk of England's batting like a bush fire, must rank high in the all-time records of sporting bravery. Greig also over-

OPPOSITE *Tony Greig, ever the adventurer! Not out of the coaching manual, but highly effective*

114

came the handicap of being an epileptic, a fact that only a few inside the game knew. Never once did he use his disability as an excuse, even after a bad day. He was in the mould of the cavalry captain who gave his orders from the front, where the flak was thickest. It was wholly in character that he would emerge as the players' spokesman justifying the Packer circus.

An articulate, intelligent man with a typically South African mercenary attitude to his chosen profession, Tony never gives less than his best, on or off the field. He made a hundred on his debut for Sussex in 1966 against Lancashire, in whose ranks was Brian Statham, then in the twilight of a magnificent career but still a fine bowler. Defensively Greig uses his considerable height to good effect, lunging out a vast distance to kill both the spin and the bounce of the ball. Like all lofty men he is happier playing forward – on the back foot the rather long pick-up and looseness always inherent in over-tall people often proves his undoing against the world's quickest bowlers.

He is at his best in attacking situations where, hitting the ball powerfully on the rise, something often possible on the near-perfect wickets found in Test cricket, he is able to keep the score galloping along. He favours the off side, again because his height makes him fall over balls pitched on his leg stump. Temperamentally he seemed to grow even more in stature, if that were possible, when England faced a crisis. He usually batted at number 6, the ideal place for an all-rounder, for it meant that when he came to the wicket there was always a specialist batsman at the other end, while behind him there were usually one or two useful tailenders to give him support.

Greig was far and away a better batsman than a bowler, yet he had one precious commodity without which he would on many occasions have been taken apart – he was lucky. His height made accuracy and control a difficult problem for him. This was less apparent when he bowled his fast-medium seamers but shone through whenever he turned to off-spin. Despite his one glorious Test against the West Indies at Port of Spain, when on a dusty wicket he returned match figures of 13 for 156, Greig was never

116

truly happy in this slower style. Indeed only Gary Sobers has ever been of Test class in more than one type of bowling. But from his great height Greig always made the ball bounce a little more than the batsman expected, and this more than anything else probably explains why he was able to come on and get a wicket after the front-line bowlers had tried in vain for a breakthrough.

Greig's tremendous body whip which, allied to his six-foot-seven-inch height, enables him to get a steep bounce off the pitch

117

As a close fielder he was fit to rank with the best of all time. Carrying very little unnecessary weight, he was able to use his length to reach slip catches that no other man would have got near. Despite his long legs he was exceptionally agile, and his pigeon-toedness helped him push off rapidly in the direction the ball had been edged. At Test match level he also brought the short square point position on the off side back into the game. At times he fielded so close that a mere stretching out of his arm would have enabled him to touch the batsman. His catching was safe and sure, both to his left and right, and the size of his hands and very long fingers helped him to hang on to the fastest travelling snick.

118

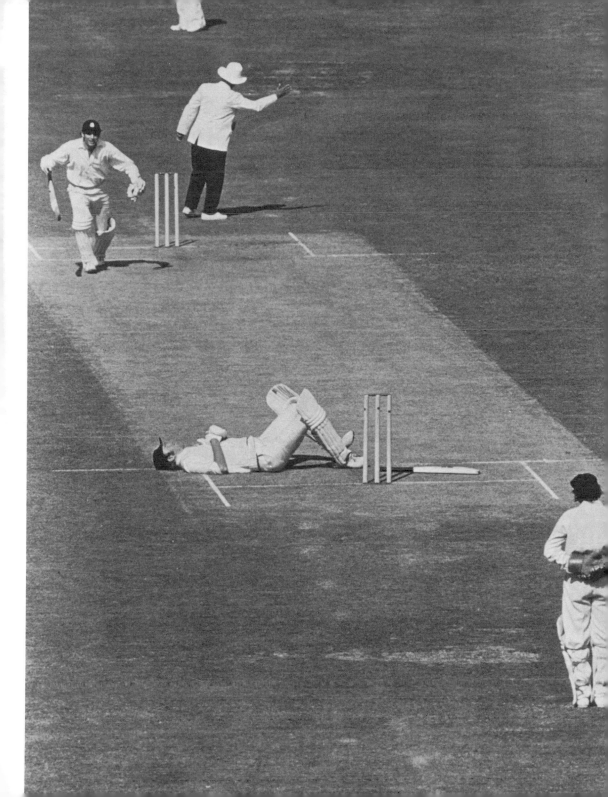

As a Test captain Greig did not rate very highly tactically. Inside the game he had many critics, but he was a quick learner, and even at the end of his fourteen-match stay as captain of England he was never above seeking or taking advice from those he respected in the game – Ray Illingworth and Brian Close for instance. He was a superb leader of a touring team, particularly to the Indian sub-continent, where his charisma entranced millions who forgot his South African background in the blaze of his extrovert personality.

Above all else, Tony Greig represents the determination factor in getting to the top as a cricketer. Few have had a more unswerving belief in their own ability to see things through to the death.

Test matches	Runs	HS	100s	Av.	Wickets	Av.	Catches
58	3599	148	8	40.43	141	32.20	87